· T R O P H I E S ·

Reading and Language Skills Assessment

Including Mid-Year and End-of-Year Assessments

Grade 6 · Teacher's Edition

Senior Author

Dr. Roger C. Farr

Chancellor's Professor and Director of
The Center for Innovation in Assessment,
Indiana University, Bloomington

Harcourt

Orlando   Boston   Dallas   Chicago   San Diego

Visit *The Learning Site!*
www.harcourtschool.com

ISBN 0-15-324966-8

3 4 5 6 7 8 9 10   170   10 09 08 07 06 05 04 03 02

Harcourt • Reading and Language Skills Assessment

Table of Contents

Appendix

· ·

Trophies
Assessment Components

∙∙

The chart below gives a brief overview of the assessment choices that are available at this grade level. The titles in boldface can be found in this Teacher's Edition.

Entry-Level Assessments	**To plan instruction**
Placement and Diagnostic Assessments	◆ To determine the best placement for a student and to diagnose strengths and weaknesses
Reading and Language Skills Pretests	◆ To determine a student's proficiency with selected skills *before* starting instruction
Formative Assessments	**To monitor student progress**
End-of-Selection Tests	◆ To monitor a student's comprehension of each selection
Oral Reading Fluency Assessment	◆ To monitor how automatically a student applies decoding skills
Assessment notes at "point of use" in the Teacher's Edition	◆ To monitor selected skills and strategies as they are taught
Mid-Year Reading and Language Skills Assessment	◆ To monitor how well a student has retained reading and language skills
Summative Assessments	**To assess mastery of skills taught** **To assess ability to apply skills and strategies**
Reading and Language Skills Posttests	◆ To assess mastery of reading and language skills taught in a theme
Holistic Assessment	◆ To evaluate a student's ability to apply reading and writing skills and strategies to new situations
End-of-Year Reading and Language Skills Assessment	◆ To evaluate mastery of reading and language skills taught during the year

Overview of the Teacher's Edition

This Teacher's Edition is organized into two major sections. Each section contains information about a separate assessment component. The two assessment components are as follows:

Reading and Language Skills Assessments

Two parallel forms of the *Reading and Language Skills Assessments*, a Pretest and a Posttest, are available for each theme at this grade. These assessments evaluate the specific skills taught in the themes. The assessments can be used in tandem before and after instruction in the theme, or they can be used independently. For example, only the posttest could be used to evaluate how well students learned the skills taught in the theme.

Mid-Year and End-of-Year Skills Assessments

Two cumulative assessments are also included in this Teacher's Edition. The *Mid-Year Reading and Language Skills Assessment* evaluates the skills taught in the first half of the year in Themes 1 through 3. The *End-of-Year Reading and Language Skills Assessment* evaluates the skills taught during the entire year in Themes 1 through 6.

Copying masters for all of the assessment booklets are located in the Appendix. They are organized as follows:

Theme 1   *Reading and Language Skills Assessment*
Theme 2   *Reading and Language Skills Assessment*
Theme 3   *Reading and Language Skills Assessment*
Mid-Year   *Reading and Language Skills Assessment*

Theme 4   *Reading and Language Skills Assessment*
Theme 5   *Reading and Language Skills Assessment*
Theme 6   *Reading and Language Skills Assessment*
End-of-Year Reading and Language Skills Assessment

Reading and Language Skills Assessments

Description of the Assessments

The *Reading and Language Skills Assessments* are criterion-referenced tests designed to measure students' achievement on the skills taught in each of the themes. Criterion-referenced scores help teachers make decisions regarding the type of additional instruction that students may need.

Six *Reading and Language Skills Assessments* are available at this grade level—one assessment for each theme. The assessments evaluate students' achievement in decoding, vocabulary, literary response and analysis, comprehension, research and information skills, and language. The formats used on the *Reading and Language Skills Assessments* follow the same style as those used in instruction. This ensures that the assessments are aligned with the instruction.

Scheduling the Assessments

The *Reading and Language Skills Assessments* have been designed to correlate with specific skills introduced and reinforced within each theme of the program. Therefore, a *Reading and Language Skills Assessment Pretest* could be administered before a theme is started to determine which skills need to be emphasized. Or, a *Reading and Language Skills Assessment Posttest* could be administered after a theme is completed to verify that students can apply the skills that were taught.

If possible, a *Reading and Language Skills Assessment* should be given in one session. The pace at which you administer the assessment will depend on your particular class and group. The assessments are not timed. Most students should be able to complete an assessment in thirty to forty-five minutes.

Directions for Administering

Accommodations can be made for students with special needs (e.g., special education, ELL). If accommodations are made for a student, they should be noted in the space provided on the cover of the assessment booklet.

Prior to administering a *Reading and Language Skills Assessment*, the following general directions should be read to the students.

Say: *Today you will be answering questions about some of the things we have learned together in class. Do your very best and try to answer each of the questions.*

When administering the assessment, repeat or clarify items that students do not hear or directions that they do not understand, but do not permit such explanations to reveal any answers.

The directions for each assessment are printed on the pages of the assessment booklets. There are no additional directions. If you wish, you may have students read the directions silently by themselves, or you may choose to read the directions aloud while students read them silently. Remember, if necessary, you may clarify any directions that students do not understand, as long as the clarification does not reveal any answers. Allow enough time for all students to complete the assessment or portion of the assessment being administered.

Scoring and Interpreting the Assessments

The *Reading and Language Skills Assessment* can be scored using the answer keys. Follow these steps:

1. Turn to the appropriate answer key in the Appendix.

2. Compare the student's responses, item by item, to the answer key and put a check mark next to each item that is correctly answered.

3. Count the number of correct responses for each skill or subtest and write this number on the "Pupil Score" line on the booklet cover. Add the Pupil Scores for each skill to obtain the Total Score.

4. Determine if the student met the criterion for each skill.

A student who scores at or above the criterion level for each subtest is considered competent in that skill area and is probably ready to move forward without additional practice. A column for writing comments about "Pupil Strength" has been provided on the cover of the assessment booklet.

A student who does not reach criterion level probably needs additional instruction and/or practice in that particular skill. Examine the student's scores for each subtest and decide whether you should reteach a particular skill, or move forward to the next theme.

For teachers who wish to keep a cumulative record of Pupil Scores across themes, a Student Record Form has been provided for that purpose in the Appendix.

A *Reading and Language Skills Assessment* is just one observation of a student's reading behavior. It should be combined with other evidence of a student's progress, such as the teacher's daily observations, student work samples, and individual reading conferences. The sum of all of this information, coupled with test scores, is more reliable and valid than any single piece of information.

Mid-Year and End-of-Year Reading and Language Skills Assessments

....

Description of the Assessments

The *Mid-Year* and *End-of-Year Reading and Language Skills Assessments* are criterion-referenced tests designed to measure students' achievement on the skills taught in the themes. The assessments evaluate students' achievement in decoding, vocabulary, literary response and analysis, comprehension, research and information skills, and language. The assessments are designed to give a global picture of how well students apply the skills taught in the program. They are not intended to be diagnostic tests and do not yield specific scores for each skill. However, if a student does not reach the overall criterion for the total test, it is possible to judge his or her performance on the major skill categories (e.g., decoding, vocabulary, and comprehension).

The formats used on the *Mid-Year* and *End-of-Year Reading and Language Skills Assessments* follow the same style as those used in instruction. This ensures that the assessments are aligned with the instruction.

Contents of the Assessments

The following tables list the contents of the *Mid-Year* and *End-of-Year Assessments*. The contents of the *Mid-Year Reading and Language Skills Assessment* come from the skills taught in Themes 1, 2, and 3. The contents of the *End-of-Year Reading and Language Skills Assessment* come from the skills taught in Themes 1 through 6.

Mid-Year Reading and Language Skills Assessment

Skill Category	Subcategory	Objective	Items
Vocabulary and Concepts	Prefixes, Suffixes, and Roots	Use prefixes, suffixes, and roots to determine or clarify word meaning	1–4
Comprehension	Sequential Structure	Recognize and analyze text that is presented in sequential or chronological order	5–8
Comprehension	Summarize and Paraphrase	Recognize a summary and a paraphrase of a passage	13, 14
Comprehension	Text Structure: Main Idea and Details	Use text structure to identify the supporting details in a passage	9–12
Literary Response and Analysis	Narrative Elements	Understand setting, theme, character development, conflict, and resolution in a story	15–18
Literary Response and Analysis	Point of View	Recognize the point of view of a narrative	19, 20
Literary Response and Analysis	Figurative Language	Identify and analyze figures of speech	21, 22
Research and Information Skills	Locate Information	Use structural features of various sources to locate information	23, 24
Research and Information Skills	Graphic Aids	Interpret information presented in multiple formats	25–28
Language		Display command of standard English conventions	29–40

End-of-Year Reading and Language Skills Assessment

Skill Category	Subcategory	Objective	Items
Vocabulary and Concepts	Prefixes, Suffixes, and Roots	Use prefixes, suffixes, and roots to determine or clarify word meaning	1, 2
Vocabulary	Word Relationships	Understand how words are related and use context to determine word meaning	3–6
Vocabulary	Denotation/ Connotation	Discriminate shades of meaning	7, 8
Comprehension	Text Structure: Main Idea and Details	Use text structure to identify the main idea and supporting details in a passage	18, 19
Comprehension	Text Structure: Compare and Contrast	Recognize and analyze text presented in a compare/contrast format	9, 12, 22–24
Comprehension	Author's Purpose and Perspective	Recognize an author's purpose and perspective	13, 17
Comprehension	Draw Conclusions	Use information from a reading selection and prior knowledge to form or support a conclusion	20, 21
Comprehension	Text Structure: Cause and Effect	Analyze cause-and-effect relationships in text	14–16
Comprehension	Fact and Opinion	Distinguish between fact and opinion	10, 11
Literary Response and Analysis	Narrative Elements	Understand setting, theme, character development, conflict, and resolution in a story	25–28
Literary Response and Analysis	Figurative Language	Identify and analyze figures of speech	29–32
Research and Information Skills	Graphic Aids	Interpret information presented in multiple formats	33–36
Language		Display command of standard English conventions	37–50

Scheduling the Assessments

The *Mid-Year* and *End-of-Year Reading and Language Skills Assessments* have been designed to correlate with specific skills introduced and reinforced within each theme of the program. Each major reading skill taught in the program is represented on the assessments. The *Mid-Year* and *End-of-Year Reading Skills Assessments* are summative tests. That is, they are designed to evaluate whether students can apply the skills learned.

The *Mid-Year Reading and Language Skills Assessment* may be given after a student has completed the first three themes of instruction at this grade level. The *End-of-Year Reading and Language Skills Assessment* may be given after a student has completed the last three themes of instruction or the entire book.

The *Mid-Year* and *End-of-Year Reading and Language Skills Assessments* should be given in one session, if possible. The pace at which you administer the assessments will depend on your particular class and group. The assessments are not timed. Most students should be able to complete each assessment in approximately forty-five minutes to an hour.

Directions for Administering

Prior to administering the *Mid-Year* and *End-of-Year Reading and Language Skills Assessments*, the following general directions should be read to the students.

Say: *Today you will be answering questions about some of the things we have learned together in class. Do your very best and try to answer each of the questions.*

Distribute the assessment booklets and have students write their names on the Name line. Then have students fold the assessment booklet so that only the page they are working on is facing up. Make sure that every student understands what to do and how to mark the answers. When testing is completed, collect the assessment booklets.

The directions for each assessment are printed on the pages of the pupil booklets. There are no additional directions. If you wish, you may have students read the directions silently by themselves, or you may choose to read the directions aloud while students read them silently. If necessary, you may clarify any directions that students do not understand, as long as the clarification does not reveal any answers. Allow enough time for all students to complete the assessment.

Scoring and Interpreting the Assessments

The *Mid-Year* and *End-of-Year Reading Skills Assessments* can be scored by using the answer keys found in the Appendix. Follow these steps:

1. Turn to the appropriate answer key in the Appendix.

2. Compare the student's responses, item by item, to the answer key, and put a check mark next to each item that is correctly answered.

3. Count the number of correct responses for each skill category and write that number on the "Pupil Score" line on the cover of the assessment booklet. Add the Pupil Scores for each skill category to obtain the student's Total Score.

4. Next, determine if the student met the criterion for Total Score. The criterion score can be found on the cover page of the assessment booklet. Use the "Interpreting Performance" chart found in this section of the Teacher's Edition booklet to interpret the student's score.

5. If a student does not reach the overall criterion on the total test, you may evaluate the student's performance on particular skill categories. Look at each skill category and determine if the student met the criterion for that skill category. Then determine the student's strengths and weaknesses for particular skill categories. Write comments in the space provided.

There are 40 items on the *Mid-Year Reading and Language Skills Assessment* and 50 on the *End-of-Year Reading and Language Skills Assessment*. For each item, a correct answer should be given 1 point, and an incorrect or missing answer should be given 0 points. Thus, a perfect score on the mid-year assessment would be 40, and a perfect score on the end-of-year assessment would be 50. Use the following performance chart to interpret score ranges.

Interpreting Performance on the
Mid-Year and *End-of-Year Reading Skills Assessments*

Total Score	Interpretation	Teaching Suggestions
Mid-Year: 29–40 **End-of-Year: 37–50**	Average to excellent understanding and use of the major reading and language skills	Students scoring at the high end of this range exceed the criterion and should have no difficulty moving forward to the next level of the program. Students scoring at the low end of this range meet the criterion and are performing at an acceptable level.
Mid-Year: 0–28 **End-of-Year: 0–36**	Fair to limited understanding and use of the major reading and language skills	Students scoring at the high end of this range are performing slightly below the criterion and may need extra help before or after moving to the next level of the program. Note whether performance varied across the skill categories tested. Examine other samples of the students' work and/or administer some of the individual assessments (e.g., Phonics Inventory, Oral Reading Fluency Assessment) to confirm their progress and pinpoint instructional needs. Students scoring at the low end of this range do not meet criterion and should have their performance verified through other measures such as some of the individual assessments available in this program, or daily work samples. Identify what specific instructional needs must be met by reviewing the student's performance on each skill category.

A student who does not reach the criterion level may not do so for a variety of reasons. Use the questions that follow to better understand why a student may not have reached the criterion.

- *Has the student completed all parts of the program being tested on the assessment?*

  If not, the results may not be valid, since the *Mid-Year Reading and Language Skills Assessment* evaluates all the major skills taught in the first three themes at this grade level, and the *End-of-Year Reading and Language Skills Assessment* evaluates all the major skills taught in Themes 1-6 at this grade level. It would be unfair to expect a student to demonstrate mastery of skills for which he or she has not received instruction.

- *Was the student having a bad day when he or she took the assessment?*

  Students can experience social or emotional problems that may affect concentration and influence performance. Sometimes a problem at home or a conflict on the school playground carries over into the classroom and interferes with performance. Recall any unusual behavior you observed before or during the testing, or confer with the student to identify any factors that may have adversely affected performance. If the student's limited performance can be attributed to extraneous problems, readminister the assessment under better conditions or discard the results.

- *Does the student perform differently on group tests than on individual tests?*

  Student performance can fluctuate depending on the context and mode of the assessment. Some students perform better in a one-on-one setting that fosters individual attention than they do in a group setting that is less personal. Others are more successful reading orally than reading silently. Likewise, some students feel more comfortable answering open-ended questions orally than they do answering multiple-choice questions on a paper-and-pencil test.

- *Does the student perform differently on tests than on daily activities?*

  Compare the student's performance on the mid-year and the end-of-year assessment with his or her performance on other formal types of assessment, such as theme tests and standardized tests. Also note how the student's performance compares with his or her performance on informal types of assessment, such as portfolios, reading logs, and anecdotal observation records. If the results are similar, it would suggest that the mid-year and the end-of-year results are valid and accurately represent the student's performance. If the results are not consistent, explore alternative explanations.

  To resolve conflicts regarding the student's performance, you may want to collect additional evidence. For example, you may want to administer some of the individual assessments available with this program (e.g., Phonics Inventory, Oral Reading Fluency Assessment).

  As with all assessments, it is important not to place too much faith in a single test. The *Mid-Year* and *End-of-Year Reading and Language Skills Assessments* are just one observation of a student's reading behavior. They should be combined with other evidence of a student's progress, such as the teacher's daily observations, the student's work samples, and individual reading conferences. The sum of all this information, combined with test scores, is more reliable and valid than any single piece of information.

Appendix

Answer Keys for *Reading and Language Skills Assessments:*
Pretests and *Posttests*
Timeless Treasures/Theme 1

PRETEST	POSTTEST
VOCABULARY: **Prefixes, Suffixes, Roots**	**VOCABULARY:** **Prefixes, Suffixes, Roots**
1. B	1. A
2. C	2. B
3. D	3. C
4. B	4. A
5. A	5. C
6. C	6. B
7. D	7. D
8. A	8. A
LITERARY RESPONSE AND ANALYSIS: **Narrative Elements**	**LITERARY RESPONSE AND ANALYSIS:** **Narrative Elements**
9. C	9. D
10. A	10. A
11. B	11. C
12. B	12. B
LANGUAGE	**LANGUAGE**
13. D	13. B
14. A	14. D
15. B	15. B
16. A	16. A
17. A	17. A
18. D	18. B
19. B	19. C
20. C	20. D
21. D	21. A
22. A	22. C

Teacher's Edition

Answer Keys for *Reading and Language Skills Assessments:* *Pretests* and *Posttests*

Timeless Treasures/Theme 2

PRETEST	POSTTEST
COMPREHENSION: **Sequential Structure**	**COMPREHENSION:** **Sequential Structure**
1. B	1. A
2. C	2. B
3. D	3. D
4. C	4. B
COMPREHENSION: **Summarize and Paraphrase**	**COMPREHENSION:** **Summarize and Paraphrase**
5. C	5. B
6. B	6. A
7. D	7. C
8. A	8. D
LITERARY RESPONSE AND ANALYSIS: **Point of View**	**LITERARY RESPONSE AND ANALYSIS:** **Point of View**
9. C	9. A
10. C	10. B
11. B	11. C
12. A	12. A
LITERARY RESPONSE AND ANALYSIS: **Figurative Language**	**LITERARY RESPONSE AND ANALYSIS:** **Figurative Language**
13. C	13. D
14. D	14. C
15. C	15. C
16. B	16. A
LANGUAGE	**LANGUAGE**
17. C	17. B
18. A	18. D
19. D	19. D
20. A	20. C
21. B	21. D
22. C	22. A
23. D	23. C
24. A	24. B
25. C	25. A
26. A	26. B

PRETEST	POSTTEST
COMPREHENSION: **Text Structure: Main Idea** **and Details** 1. C 2. A 3. B 4. C	**COMPREHENSION:** **Text Structure: Main Idea** **and Details** 1. D 2. A 3. B 4. A
RESEARCH AND **INFORMATION SKILLS:** **Locate Information** 5. A 6. C 7. C 8. B	**RESEARCH AND** **INFORMATION SKILLS:** **Locate Information** 5. B 6. D 7. A 8. B
RESEARCH AND **INFORMATION SKILLS:** **Graphic Aids** 9. A 10. B 11. C 12. C	**RESEARCH AND** **INFORMATION SKILLS:** **Graphic Aids** 9. A 10. C 11. A 12. B
LANGUAGE 13. B 14. D 15. C 16. A 17. B 18. D 19. C 20. B 21. D 22. B	**LANGUAGE** 13. D 14. A 15. A 16. D 17. C 18. B 19. A 20. B 21. C 22. A

PRETEST	POSTTEST
VOCABULARY AND CONCEPTS: Word Relationships	**VOCABULARY AND CONCEPTS: Word Relationships**
1. D	1. C
2. C	2. C
3. C	3. B
4. B	4. D
5. B	5. C
6. A	6. B
COMPREHENSION: Text Structure: Compare and Contrast	**COMPREHENSION: Text Structure: Compare and Contrast**
7. C	7. C
8. D	8. D
9. B	9. A
10. A	10. C
11. C	11. C
12. D	12. D
13. A	13. A
14. C	14. C
LANGUAGE	**LANGUAGE**
15. C	15. B
16. D	16. C
17. B	17. D
18. A	18. D
19. B	19. C
20. D	20. A
21. B	21. B
22. C	22. A
23. D	23. C
24. C	24. D

PRETEST	POSTTEST

COMPREHENSION:
Author's Purpose and
Perspective
  1. B
  2. C
  3. A
  4. B
	COMPREHENSION:
	Author's Purpose and
	Perspective
	  1. B
	  2. A
	  3. C
	  4. B

COMPREHENSION:
Draw Conclusions
  5. D
  6. B
  7. C
  8. C
  9. A
10. B
11. C
12. A
	COMPREHENSION:
	Draw Conclusions
	  5. A
	  6. D
	  7. B
	  8. C
	  9. A
	10. B
	11. A
	12. C

LANGUAGE 13. C 14. D 15. D 16. B 17. C 18. D 19. B 20. C 21. C 22. B	**LANGUAGE** 13. D 14. C 15. B 16. A 17. D 18. C 19. C 20. D 21. C 22. D

Answer Keys for *Reading and Language Skills Assessments: Pretests* and *Posttests*

Timeless Treasures/Theme 6

PRETEST	POSTTEST
VOCABULARY AND CONCEPTS: **Denotation/Connotation**	**VOCABULARY AND CONCEPTS:** **Denotation/Connotation**
1. A	1. C
2. B	2. A
3. B	3. A
4. C	4. B
COMPREHENSION: **Text Structure: Cause and Effect**	**COMPREHENSION:** **Text Structure: Cause and Effect**
5. B	5. A
6. A	6. C
7. D	7. B
8. D	8. D
COMPREHENSION: **Fact and Opinion**	**COMPREHENSION:** **Fact and Opinion**
9. C	9. D
10. B	10. A
11. A	11. B
12. B	12. C
LANGUAGE	**LANGUAGE**
13. C	13. A
14. D	14. C
15. B	15. C
16. A	16. B
17. C	17. D
18. A	18. B
19. D	19. D
20. C	20. C
21. C	21. B
22. B	22. A

Answer Key
Mid-Year Reading and Language Skills Assessment

VOCABULARY AND CONCEPTS
1. B
2. C
3. D
4. A

COMPREHENSION
5. B
6. C
7. C
8. D
9. A
10. B
11. D
12. C
13. A
14. B

LITERARY RESPONSE AND ANALYSIS
15. C
16. D
17. A
18. B
19. C
20. A
21. B
22. A

RESEARCH AND INFORMATION SKILLS
23. C
24. D
25. B
26. C
27. C
28. D

LANGUAGE
29. A
30. A
31. C
32. B
33. D
34. B
35. A
36. C
37. B
38. C
39. A
40. A

Answer Key

End-of-Year Reading and Language Skills Assessment

VOCABULARY
1. B
2. C
3. A
4. D
5. C
6. A
7. B
8. C

COMPREHENSION
9. B
10. C
11. D
12. A
13. B
14. C
15. B
16. A
17. C
18. B
19. D
20. B
21. A
22. C
23. B
24. D

LITERARY RESPONSE AND ANALYSIS
25. B
26. C
27. D
28. A
29. C
30. B
31. A
32. B

RESEARCH AND INFORMATION SKILLS
33. B
34. C
35. B
36. C

LANGUAGE
37. D
38. A
39. D
40. B
41. D
42. B
43. C
44. B
45. D
46. C
47. D
48. B
49. D
50. C

Student Record Form
Reading and Language Skills Assessment
Trophies
Grade 6

Name _____ **Grade** _____

Teacher _____

	CRITERION SCORE	PUPIL SCORE	COMMENTS
Theme 1			
Prefixes, suffixes, roots	6/8	___/8	_____
Narrative elements	3/4	___/4	_____
Language	7/10	___/10	_____
Theme 2			
Sequential structure	3/4	___/4	_____
Summarize and paraphrase	3/4	___/4	_____
Point of view	3/4	___/4	_____
Figurative language	3/4	___/4	_____
Language	7/10	___/10	_____
Theme 3			
Text Structure: Main idea and details	3/4	___/4	_____
Locate information	3/4	___/4	_____
Graphic aids	3/4	___/4	_____
Language	7/10	___/10	_____

Teacher's Edition

Student Record Form
Reading and Language Skills Assessment
Trophies
Grade 6

Name _____ **Grade** _____

Teacher _____

	CRITERION SCORE	PUPIL SCORE	COMMENTS
Theme 4			
Word Relationships	4/6	___/6	_____
Text Structure: Compare and contrast	6/8	___/8	_____
Language	7/10	___/10	_____
Theme 5			
Author's purpose and perspective	3/4	___/4	_____
Draw conclusions	6/8	___/8	_____
Language	7/10	___/10	_____
Theme 6			
Denotation/Connotation	3/4	___/4	_____
Text Structure: Cause and effect	3/4	___/4	_____
Fact and opinion	3/4	___/4	_____
Language	7/10	___/10	_____

TROPHIES

Reading and Language Skills Assessment Pretest

Timeless Treasures / Theme 1

Name _____ Date _____

SKILL AREA	Criterion Score	Pupil Score	Pupil Strength
VOCABULARY AND CONCEPTS Prefixes, Suffixes, Roots	6/8	_____	_____
LITERARY RESPONSE AND ANALYSIS Narrative Elements	3/4	_____	_____
LANGUAGE Sentences; Interjections Complete and Simple Subjects Complete and Simple Predicates Compound Subjects and Predicates Simple and Compound Sentences	7/10	_____	_____
TOTAL SCORE	16/22	_____	_____

Were accommodations made in administering this test? ☐ Yes ☐ No

Type of accommodations: _____

_____

Printed in the United States of America

ISBN 0-15-332212-8

3 4 5 6 7 8 9 10   170   10 09 08 07 06 05 04 03 02

VOCABULARY AND CONCEPTS: Prefixes, Suffixes, Roots

Directions: Fill in the answer circle in front of the correct answer for each question.

1. The travelers were forewarned about the bad weather.

   What does the word *forewarned* mean?

   Ⓐ not warned

   Ⓑ warned before

   Ⓒ warned again

   Ⓓ half warned

2. The airplane flew in a semicircle as it approached the runway.

   What does the word *semicircle* mean?

   Ⓐ two circles

   Ⓑ a bad circle

   Ⓒ a half circle

   Ⓓ circle again

3. Which prefix can be added to the word *value* to make it mean "the opposite of value"?

   Ⓐ *pre-*

   Ⓑ *bi-*

   Ⓒ *multi-*

   Ⓓ *de-*

4. The baseball game caused excitement in the spectators.

   What does the word *excitement* mean?

   Ⓐ not exciting

   Ⓑ an excited state

   Ⓒ one who excites

   Ⓓ capable of being excited

GO ON

VOCABULARY AND CONCEPTS: Prefixes, Suffixes, Roots (continued)

5. Which suffix can be added to the word *music* to make it mean "relating to music"?

Ⓐ *-al*

Ⓑ *-ful*

Ⓒ *-able*

Ⓓ *-ment*

6. Mr. Jones is my biology teacher.

What part of the word *biology* means "the study of"?

Ⓐ bio

Ⓑ biolo

Ⓒ ology

Ⓓ gy

7. Which word has the same root as *construction* and *destruct*?

Ⓐ detract

Ⓑ convince

Ⓒ object

Ⓓ structure

8. Which root means *trust*?

Ⓐ "cred" as in **credit**

Ⓑ "bene" as in **beneficial**

Ⓒ "pan" as in **panorama**

Ⓓ "tele" as in **telephone**

STOP

LITERARY RESPONSE AND ANALYSIS: Narrative Elements

Directions: Read the passage. Fill in the answer circle in front of the correct answer for each question.

"I am *not* going to school looking like this, Mom, and that's final!" Luke ran out of the kitchen, took the steps up to his room two at a time, and threw himself down on his bed. "It's official," he thought. "I'm a metal mouth. I'm never going to smile again. I hate these braces. I'm not going to open my mouth and let everyone see how goofy I look, and no one can make me. How am I ever going to survive two years of wearing these? The kids at school will make every joke in the book at my expense. It's going to be a nightmare." He decided to go to bed early so he wouldn't have to think about it.

The next morning, Luke ate breakfast, wincing to let his parents know how uncomfortable the braces were. After he brushed his teeth, he put little balls of wax on the sharp edges of the braces so they wouldn't bother him. Then he caught the bus to school.

During first period, Mrs. Evans announced that there was a new student named Lucy in the class. Luke barely paid attention until Lucy walked over and sat at the desk by his. "May I borrow a sheet of paper?" she asked. Then she gave Luke a big, friendly smile, showing her braces. Luke grinned back.

GO ON

LITERARY RESPONSE AND ANALYSIS: Narrative Elements (continued)

9. The main character in this story is _____.

(A) Mrs. Evans

(B) Lucy

(C) Luke

(D) Luke's mom

10. Why did Luke wince when he ate breakfast?

(A) to win sympathy and make his parents feel guilty

(B) to show his parents that he didn't like the breakfast food

(C) to convince his parents that the braces wouldn't straighten his teeth

(D) to amuse his parents by looking funny while he ate

11. This story takes place _____.

(A) on a weekend

(B) during the school week

(C) during the summer

(D) on a school holiday

12. The main problem in this story is that a boy _____.

(A) has trouble making friends in a new class

(B) has to get used to a change in his appearance

(C) can't convince his parents to let him make decisions

(D) is bullied by others at his school

STOP

Score _____

Harcourt • Reading and Language Skills Assessment

LANGUAGE

Directions: Choose the best answer for each question.

13. Which group of words is a **sentence**?

    (A) Suddenly pounced on its prey.

    (B) The shiny new paint job.

    (C) Dove into the cool water.

    (D) Wow, look at him go!

14. What **kind of sentence** is this?

    An *isthmus* is a narrow strip of land that connects two larger land areas.

    (A) declarative

    (B) interrogative

    (C) imperative

    (D) exclamatory

15. Which sentence has the correct **end punctuation**?

    (A) What a graceful dancer you are.

    (B) Our school is considering going to a year-round schedule.

    (C) Do you have time to help me with my math homework!

    (D) Put on your helmet before riding your mountain bike?

GO ON

LANGUAGE (continued)

Directions: Read each sentence. Choose the underlined noun that is the **simple subject** of each sentence.

16. The early <u>Egyptians</u> wore <u>shoes</u> that showed their <u>wealth</u> or <u>importance</u>.
    - (A) Egyptians
    - (B) shoes
    - (C) wealth
    - (D) importance

17. The <u>sweater</u> of soft <u>wool</u> was woven by <u>one</u> of my <u>aunts</u>.
    - (A) sweater
    - (B) wool
    - (C) one
    - (D) aunts

Directions: Read each sentence. Choose the underlined word that is the **simple predicate**, or verb, in each sentence.

18. The <u>soccer</u> team's <u>goalkeeper</u> <u>successfully</u> <u>blocked</u> the ball.
    - (A) soccer
    - (B) goalkeeper
    - (C) successfully
    - (D) blocked

19. The <u>determined</u> batter <u>swung</u> at the <u>ball</u> with all his <u>might</u>.
    - (A) determined
    - (B) swung
    - (C) ball
    - (D) might

Harcourt • Reading and Language Skills Assessment

GO ON

Timeless Treasures / Theme 1

LANGUAGE (continued)

Directions: Read each pair or group of sentences. Choose the answer that shows the best way to combine the sentences.

20. The trumpet is a brass instrument. The trombone is a brass instrument. The tuba is a brass instrument.

(A) The trumpet, trombone and tuba are brass; brass instruments.

(B) The trumpet and trombone are brass the tuba is brass.

(C) The trumpet, trombone, and tuba are brass instruments.

(D) Trumpets, trombones, and tubas, and brass instruments.

21. The skin divers checked their air tanks. The skin divers put on their flippers.

(A) The skin divers put on their tanks they checked their flippers.

(B) The skin divers checked and put on; their air tanks and flippers.

(C) The skin divers check their air tanks, the divers put on their flippers.

(D) The skin divers checked their air tanks and put on their flippers.

22. The guest speaker was interesting. The audience members didn't listen.

(A) The guest speaker was interesting, but the audience members didn't listen.

(B) The guest speaker was interesting and the audience members didn't listen.

(C) The guest speaker was interesting, or the audience members didn't listen.

(D) The guest speaker was interesting, the audience members didn't listen.

STOP

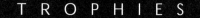
· T R O P H I E S ·

Personal Best / Theme 1
Reading and Language Skills Assessment

Harcourt

Orlando   Boston   Dallas   Chicago   San Diego

Part No. 9997-37777-X

ISBN 0-15-332212-8 (Package of 12)

6

· T R O P H I E S ·

Reading and Language Skills Assessment Posttest

Timeless Treasures / Theme 1

Name _____ Date _____

SKILL AREA	Criterion Score	Pupil Score	Pupil Strength
VOCABULARY AND CONCEPTS Prefixes, Suffixes, Roots	6/8	_____	_____
LITERARY RESPONSE AND ANALYSIS Narrative Elements	3/4	_____	_____
LANGUAGE Sentences; Interjections Complete and Simple Subjects Complete and Simple Predicates Compound Subjects and Predicates Simple and Compound Sentences	7/10	_____	_____
TOTAL SCORE	16/22	_____	_____

Were accommodations made in administering this test? ❑ Yes ❑ No

Type of accommodations: _____

_____

VOCABULARY: Prefixes, Suffixes, Roots

Directions: Fill in the answer circle in front of the correct answer for each question.

1. We went on a transcontinental trip for our vacation.

   What does the word *transcontinental* mean?

   (A) across the continent

   (B) below the continent

   (C) into the continent

   (D) middle of the continent

2. Someday, interplanetary travel will be a routine occurrence.

   What does the word *interplanetary* mean?

   (A) over planets

   (B) between planets

   (C) under planets

   (D) many planets

3. Which prefix can be added to the word *told* to make it mean "told before"?

   (A) *un-*

   (B) *non-*

   (C) *fore-*

   (D) *mis-*

4. Christmas is a time for familial harmony.

   What does the word *familial* mean?

   (A) relating to family

   (B) able to be family

   (C) without family

   (D) cause to be family

GO ON

VOCABULARY: Prefixes, Suffixes, Roots (continued)

5. Which suffix can be added to the word *develop* to make it mean "the act of developing"?

Ⓐ *-or*

Ⓑ *-ful*

Ⓒ *-ment*

Ⓓ *-able*

6. Governor Macy has very good diction.

What part of the word *diction* means "speak"?

Ⓐ di

Ⓑ dict

Ⓒ tion

Ⓓ on

7. Which word has the same root as *tractor* and *traction*?

Ⓐ tragedy

Ⓑ trade

Ⓒ motion

Ⓓ attraction

8. Which root means *earth*?

Ⓐ "geo" as in **geography**

Ⓑ "therm" as in **thermal**

Ⓒ "miss" as in **transmission**

Ⓓ "scope" as in **periscope**

STOP

Score _____   *Timeless Treasures / Theme 1*

Harcourt • Reading and Language Skills Assessment

LITERARY RESPONSE AND ANALYSIS: Narrative Elements

Directions: Read the passage. Fill in the answer circle in front of the correct answer for each question.

It was late Saturday morning by the time the Lopez family pulled up in front of their new house. Their car was loaded with an assortment of clothes, sports equipment, and boxes that they had packed earlier that morning. The moving van would arrive at any time. Everything was settled except for one thing—which bedroom each child would get.

Maria and Gary both wanted the same bedroom—the large one on the second floor with a window overlooking the park. Maria argued that since she was older, she should get first choice, and the big bedroom was definitely her choice. "Besides," she said, "I can have my friends over for slumber parties, and we can all share the same room."

"I don't care about your slumber parties," grumbled Gary. "I have all my electronic gear to worry about—my computer, my stereo, my speakers, and my TV. I need the extra space to store all of my equipment. I deserve that room!" yelled Gary, as he slammed the car door and stomped up to the house.

Maria wouldn't budge. She insisted SHE deserved the room because she was older. Gary would just have to find another place to store his equipment.

After unlocking the door, Mr. Lopez put his arm around Gary's shoulder and said, "Let's go check on the doghouse in the backyard."

When they reached the backyard, Gary and his father sat down to talk. "Son, I have an idea. Why don't you let your sister take the big bedroom that she wants? In exchange, we will set up a special section of the family room for your stereo and speakers. You can have your friends over anytime to listen to music. You will actually have more space in the family room than you would have in the big bedroom anyway. Your computer and TV will fit in the smaller bedroom. What do you think?"

"I'm not thrilled with your suggestion," grumbled Gary, "but I guess it's not a bad compromise. I'll start bringing my stereo into the family room."

GO ON

LITERARY RESPONSE AND ANALYSIS: Narrative Elements (continued)

9. In this story, Gary is _____.
   - (A) quiet and shy
   - (B) calm and rational
   - (C) lonely and bored
   - (D) angry and argumentative

10. The setting of this story is _____.
    - (A) Saturday morning at the Lopez family's new house
    - (B) the first day of school in a new neighborhood
    - (C) a slumber party in Maria's new bedroom
    - (D) Sunday morning in the park

11. The problem in this story concerns a _____.
    - (A) quarrel about a stereo
    - (B) fight about having friends over
    - (C) dispute over a bedroom
    - (D) problem with the moving van

12. How is the problem in this story resolved?
    - (A) Mr. Lopez makes Gary give all his electronic gear to Maria.
    - (B) Maria gets the large bedroom, and Gary puts his stereo and speakers in the family room.
    - (C) Mr. Lopez tells Maria and Gary not to invite friends over for slumber parties or to listen to music.
    - (D) The movers agree to help unpack all of the Lopez family's boxes.

STOP

Score _____

Harcourt • Reading and Language Skills Assessment

LANGUAGE

Directions: Choose the best answer for each question.

13. Which group of words is a **sentence**?

Ⓐ A great opportunity for me.

Ⓑ I'd rather walk than ride the bus.

Ⓒ Bolted out of the open gate.

Ⓓ Calmly watched from a distance.

14. What **kind of sentence** is this?

You should have seen the huge yellow diamond!

Ⓐ declarative

Ⓑ interrogative

Ⓒ imperative

Ⓓ exclamatory

15. Which sentence has the correct **end punctuation**?

Ⓐ The word *planets* is from the Greek word meaning "wanderers"?

Ⓑ Have you gathered the materials you need for the project?

Ⓒ Matter is anything that has mass and takes up space!

Ⓓ Golly, that guy is actually going to pick up the deadly snake.

GO ON

LANGUAGE (continued)

Directions: Read each sentence. Choose the underlined noun that is the **simple subject** of each sentence.

16. The <u>weight</u> of an <u>object</u> is related to the <u>force</u> of <u>gravity</u>.
    - Ⓐ weight
    - Ⓑ object
    - Ⓒ force
    - Ⓓ gravity

17. The old metal <u>shed</u> in the <u>backyard</u> is coated with <u>rust</u> and <u>dirt</u>.
    - Ⓐ shed
    - Ⓑ backyard
    - Ⓒ rust
    - Ⓓ dirt

Directions: Read each sentence. Choose the underlined word that is the **simple predicate,** or verb, in each sentence.

18. Your <u>eyes</u> <u>work</u> in the <u>same</u> way as a <u>camera</u>.
    - Ⓐ eyes
    - Ⓑ work
    - Ⓒ same
    - Ⓓ camera

19. The <u>brave</u> <u>young</u> child <u>sat</u> <u>quietly</u> as the nurse bandaged her arm.
    - Ⓐ brave
    - Ⓑ young
    - Ⓒ sat
    - Ⓓ quietly

GO ON ▶

LANGUAGE (continued)

Directions: Read each pair or group of sentences. Choose the answer that shows the best way to combine the sentences.

20. Trees provide shade. Trees help keep our air clean.

Ⓐ Trees provide shade trees help keep our air clean.

Ⓑ Trees provide and help keep shade; our air clean,

Ⓒ Trees provide shade, Trees help keep our air clean.

Ⓓ Trees provide shade and help keep our air clean.

21. Oranges contain Vitamin C. Carrots contain Vitamin A.

Ⓐ Oranges contain Vitamin C, and carrots contain Vitamin A.

Ⓑ Oranges contain Vitamin C or carrots contain Vitamin A.

Ⓒ Oranges contain Vitamin C but, carrots contain Vitamin A.

Ⓓ Oranges , carrots, and they contain Vitamin C and Vitamin A.

22. Riding in a car pool helps reduce air pollution. People prefer to drive alone.

Ⓐ Riding in a car pool helps reduce air pollution, people prefer to drive alone.

Ⓑ Riding in a car pool helps reduce air pollution and, people prefer to drive alone.

Ⓒ Riding in a car pool helps reduce air pollution, but people prefer to drive alone.

Ⓓ Riding in a car pool helps reduce air pollution or people prefer to drive alone.

STOP

TROPHIES

Personal Best / Theme 1
Reading and Language Skills Assessment

Harcourt

Orlando   Boston   Dallas   Chicago   San Diego

Part No. 9997-37771-0

ISBN 0-15-332212-8 (Package of 12)

6

TROPHIES

Reading and Language Skills Assessment Pretest

Timeless Treasures / Theme 2

Name _____ Date _____

SKILL AREA	Criterion Score	Pupil Score	Pupil Strength
COMPREHENSION			
Sequential Structure	3/4	_____	_____
Summarize and Paraphrase	3/4	_____	_____
LITERARY RESPONSE AND ANALYSIS			
Point of View	3/4	_____	_____
Figurative Language	3/4	_____	_____
LANGUAGE	7/10	_____	_____
Complex Sentences			
Compound-Complex Sentences			
Common and Proper Nouns; Abbreviations			
Singular and Plural Nouns			
Possessive Nouns			
TOTAL SCORE	19/26	_____	_____

Were accommodations made in administering this test? ☐ Yes ☐ No

Type of accommodations: _____

_____

Printed in the United States of America

ISBN 0-15-332212-8

3 4 5 6 7 8 9 10   170   10 09 08 07 06 05 04 03 02

COMPREHENSION: Sequential Structure

Directions: Read each passage. Fill in the answer circle in front of the correct answer for each question.

We have all seen lightning and heard thunder. During a thunderstorm, the bottoms of clouds carry mainly a negative electrical charge. These negative charges cause the surface of the earth below to become positively charged. When this difference becomes large enough, charges rapidly move from the cloud to the earth. As this happens, we see a flash of light, which we call lightning.

When lightning strikes, it heats the surrounding air and causes the air to expand rapidly. This produces the cracking sound that we call thunder.

If lightning and thunder are produced at the same time, why do we see lightning before we hear thunder? The answer is simple. Light travels more than 880,000 times as fast as sound, so the flash from lightning reaches your eyes before the sound of thunder reaches your ears.

1. In the opening paragraph of this passage, the author _____.
   - Ⓐ gives an opinion about thunderstorms and supports it with convincing evidence
   - Ⓑ tells how lightning is produced, giving the events in the order they occur
   - Ⓒ describes differences and similarities between lightning and thunder
   - Ⓓ tells about problems caused by lightning and gives solutions for the problems

2. During a thunderstorm, a person will **first** _____.
   - Ⓐ hear the crack of thunder
   - Ⓑ feel the air expand
   - Ⓒ see the flash of lightning
   - Ⓓ feel the ground shake

GO ON

COMPREHENSION: Sequential Structure (continued)

> The food that the first astronauts ate as they traveled in space was not very tasty. Some foods were freeze-dried and cut into bite-sized cubes. Other meals had to be squeezed out of tubes like toothpaste. Because there is no gravity in space, loose pieces of food or drops of liquid could float around the ship and damage the instruments. The people planning the astronauts' diet had to keep this in mind.
>
> The astronauts were not happy about their limited meal choices. However, things soon improved. New kinds of containers were invented. The astronauts in Gemini spacecraft ate chicken and vegetables, applesauce, and pudding. Later, on the Apollo spacecraft, the astronauts had hot water for the first time. They could mix the hot water with their freeze-dried food to make it taste better.
>
> Today's astronauts stay in space much longer than the first astronauts did. They need to eat well to stay strong and healthy. Space shuttle astronauts choose their own meals and snacks before they take off. There is a great variety of food to choose from, including cereal or eggs for breakfast, macaroni and cheese, and tortillas. On the ship, the astronauts have water to mix with their food and an oven to warm it. There is no refrigerator on the shuttle, so all of the fresh fruits and vegetables must be eaten in the first few days of the trip.
>
> The space shuttle may not be the finest restaurant in the world, but it might just be the finest restaurant *out* of the world!

3. The author organizes the entire passage by _____.

Ⓐ giving detailed steps for making each type of food

Ⓑ expressing an opinion about space travel and giving convincing support

Ⓒ listing the foods that were used by the very first astronauts

Ⓓ telling how astronauts' food has changed over time, from past to present

4. Which event occurred **first**?

Ⓐ Astronauts were given a variety of foods.

Ⓑ An oven was put on a spacecraft.

Ⓒ Astronauts squeezed food from tubes.

Ⓓ Hot water became available on spacecrafts.

STOP

Harcourt • Reading and Language Skills Assessment

COMPREHENSION: Summarize and Paraphrase

Directions: Read each passage. Fill in the answer circle in front of the correct answer for each question.

The new community center was officially opening. Julia felt proud as she watched the mayor and other important people from the town getting ready to cut the ribbon and make speeches. She recalled how she and her classmates had written letters and met with town leaders to convince them that a new community center was needed. It was Mr. Evans, her social studies teacher, who had convinced the class that they could have an effect on important decisions. They needed only to select a worthwhile cause and to labor diligently on its behalf.

As Julia listened to speeches and felt the excitement of the audience, she was glad she and her classmates had accepted the challenge to become involved in community affairs.

5. What is the best summary of this passage?

Ⓐ The mayor and other important people from the town cut a ribbon and made speeches, thanks to Mr. Evans's class.

Ⓑ Mr. Evans convinced Julia and her classmates that they could have an effect on important decisions. They wrote letters to town leaders.

Ⓒ At the ribbon-cutting ceremony for the new community center, Julia proudly remembered how she and her classmates, who had been inspired by Mr. Evans to become involved in the community, convinced town leaders to build the center.

Ⓓ Julia watched as the ribbon was being cut as part of the ceremony that would officially open the town's new community center to the public. The mayor was there, and Julia felt the excitement of the audience.

6. What is the best paraphrase of the last sentence of paragraph 1?

Ⓐ They needed to find something good to do.

Ⓑ All they had to do was choose a good cause and work to support it.

Ⓒ She and her classmates needed to get busy.

Ⓓ Mr. Evans didn't care what they did as long as they got to work.

GO ON

COMPREHENSION: Summarize and Paraphrase (continued)

The West African plains, called *savannas*, are covered with stiff grasses and clumps of trees. They contain magnificent herds of grazing animals as well as deadly predators, such as the lion, which springs at its prey in a short, bounding rush. Savannas are located near the equator, and they have periods of heavy rainfall followed by periods of drought.

Savanna plants are adapted for survival. They have large underground root systems that help them survive fires and lack of water during the dry season. The coarse grasses have vertical leaves that further help them conserve water. An adaptation of some trees and shrubs—thorns or sharp leaves—discourages hungry herbivores.

Animals are likewise adapted to their environment. Grazing animals, such as the impala and wildebeest, follow the rains to areas of newly sprouted grass. Many savanna animals give birth only during the rainy season, when food is most plentiful. Herbivores reduce competition for food by feeding on vegetation at different heights. For example, small gazelles eat grasses, and giraffes feed on tree leaves.

7. Which of these ideas is most important to include in a summary of this passage?

Ⓐ The lion springs at its prey in a short rush.

Ⓑ Impala and wildebeest are grazing animals.

Ⓒ Savanna grasses are coarse and stiff.

Ⓓ Plants on the savanna are adapted for survival.

8. What is the best paraphrase of the last sentence of paragraph 2?

Ⓐ Some trees and shrubs have thorns or sharp leaves that keep herbivores from eating them.

Ⓑ Another adaptation of plants on the savanna is the presence of thorns and sharp leaves.

Ⓒ Some herbivores are hungry for thorns and sharp leaves.

Ⓓ Herbivores eat plants, and thorny and sharp trees and shrubs are plants.

Harcourt • Reading and Language Skills Assessment

STOP

Score _____

LITERARY RESPONSE AND ANALYSIS: Point of View

Directions: Read each passage. Fill in the answer circle in front of the correct answer for each question.

The noise level in the school cafeteria was somewhere between a jet plane taking off and a volcano erupting. Jason and his friends, Noah and Xavier, laughed and joked with each other as they ate. The truth was that none of them could really hear or understand what the other two were saying. That didn't stop them from carrying on like a flock of chattering birds.

9. Which point of view does the author use to tell this story?
   Ⓐ First person
   Ⓑ Third-person limited (to Jason's view)
   Ⓒ Third-person omniscient (all-knowing)
   Ⓓ There is not enough evidence in the passage to identify the point of view.

10. Which sentence, if added to the story, would show the same point of view?
   Ⓐ Then we all decided to go outside to the playground.
   Ⓑ I tried to ask Noah if I could borrow a pencil for math class.
   Ⓒ The boys enjoyed each other's company at lunch each day.
   Ⓓ All too soon, the bell will ring and our lunch period will be over.

GO ON

LITERARY RESPONSE AND ANALYSIS: Point of View (continued)

In the championship tennis match, Denise won the first game of the set. I knew I had to win the next game, or else she would have me in deep trouble. Denise was famous for beating her opponents easily. A player could not let her get too far ahead and still hope to make a comeback against her. She was a determined and confident player.

11. Which group of words from the passage shows the first-person point of view?

(A) In the championship tennis match . . .

(B) I knew I had to win . . .

(C) A player could not let her get . . .

(D) . . . a determined and confident player . . .

Tim stood at the free throw line, ready to take his shots. If he could sink both baskets, the score would be tied. He knew that everyone was looking at him. He wondered what his teammates would think of him if he missed.

12. Which sentence expresses the same point of view as the passage?

(A) Tim felt his pulse quicken with excitement and nerves.

(B) If I can make these shots, our team has a chance to win.

(C) I wish I had spent more time practicing free throws!

(D) All I can do is try my best and see what happens.

STOP

Score _____

Harcourt • Reading and Language Skills Assessment

LITERARY RESPONSE AND ANALYSIS: Figurative Language

Directions: Read the passage. Fill in the answer circle in front of the correct answer for each question.

Today was no day to be on the water. The sky was gray, and the wind howled in anger. The waves were walls, pushing boats back toward land. The fishermen stood on the dock, gear in hand. They grumbled about losing a day's pay, but they knew that staying home was the right decision.

13. Which group of words in this passage is an example of personification?

Ⓐ Today was no day . . .

Ⓑ The sky was gray . . .

Ⓒ . . . wind howled in anger.

Ⓓ They grumbled . . .

14. The passage says that the "waves were walls" because the waves were _____.

Ⓐ flat

Ⓑ solid

Ⓒ shaped like squares

Ⓓ high and strong

GO ON

LITERARY RESPONSE AND ANALYSIS: Figurative Language (continued)

Directions: Read each sentence. Fill in the answer circle in front of the correct answer for each question.

15. **The sad sky wept tears of rain.**
   This is an example of _____.
   Ⓐ a metaphor
   Ⓑ a simile
   Ⓒ personification
   Ⓓ hyperbole

16. **The racers sprang forward like arrows shot from bows.**
   This is an example of _____.
   Ⓐ a metaphor
   Ⓑ a simile
   Ⓒ personification
   Ⓓ hyperbole

STOP

Score _____   *Timeless Treasures / Theme 2*

Harcourt • Reading and Language Skills Assessment

LANGUAGE

Directions: Choose the answer that best describes the underlined words in each sentence.

17. <u>When a volcano explodes</u>, hot gases and ash fly up into the sky.
    - Ⓐ independent clause
    - Ⓑ compound sentence
    - Ⓒ dependent clause
    - Ⓓ coordinating conjunction

18. <u>The weather forecasters were alarmed</u> because the storm was growing stronger.
    - Ⓐ independent clause
    - Ⓑ complex sentence
    - Ⓒ compound sentence
    - Ⓓ dependent clause

19. <u>As the hurricane grew in strength, the police began to evacuate the town; some people refused to leave.</u>
    - Ⓐ independent clause
    - Ⓑ complex sentence
    - Ⓒ compound sentence
    - Ⓓ compound-complex sentence

Directions: Read the pair of sentences. Choose the answer that shows the best way to combine the sentences to form a complex sentence.

20. Sharks live in all parts of the ocean. They are most often found in warm waters.
    - Ⓐ Although sharks live in all parts of the ocean, they are most often found in warm waters.
    - Ⓑ Sharks live in all parts of the ocean; most often found in warm waters.
    - Ⓒ Sharks live in all parts of the ocean since they are most often found; in warm waters.
    - Ⓓ Before sharks live in all parts of the ocean and warm waters, sharks are often found.

GO ON

LANGUAGE (continued)

Directions: Read each sentence. Choose the proper noun or abbreviation that should be capitalized in each.

21. In the <u>country</u> of <u>argentina</u>, <u>cowboys</u> called *gauchos* tend large <u>herds</u> of cattle.
    Ⓐ country
    Ⓑ argentina
    Ⓒ cowboys
    Ⓓ herds

22. The <u>winner</u> of the <u>international</u> science award, <u>dr.</u> Ericson, will speak at our local <u>college</u>.
    Ⓐ winner
    Ⓑ international
    Ⓒ dr.
    Ⓓ college

Directions: Choose the plural noun that is written correctly.

23. Ⓐ boxs
    Ⓑ ladys
    Ⓒ husbandes
    Ⓓ halves

24. Ⓐ deer
    Ⓑ potatos
    Ⓒ dishs
    Ⓓ childs

GO ON

LANGUAGE (continued)

Directions: Choose the correct possessive noun to complete each sentence.

25. My best _____ father has agreed to be our soccer coach.
    - (A) friends's
    - (B) friends
    - (C) friend's
    - (D) friends'

26. Our governor received more than 65 percent of the vote, so he is clearly the _____ choice.
    - (A) people's
    - (B) people
    - (C) peoples's
    - (D) peoples

STOP

· T R O P H I E S ·

Friends to the Rescue / Theme 2
Reading and Language Skills Assessment

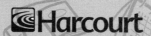

Orlando   Boston   Dallas   Chicago   San Diego

Part No. 9997-37778-8

ISBN 0-15-332212-8 (Package of 12)

6

· T R O P H I E S ·

Reading and Language Skills
Assessment Posttest

Timeless Treasures / Theme 2

Name _____ Date _____

SKILL AREA	Criterion Score	Pupil Score	Pupil Strength
COMPREHENSION			
Sequential Structure	3/4	_____	_____
Summarize and Paraphrase	3/4	_____	_____
LITERARY RESPONSE AND ANALYSIS			
Point of View	3/4	_____	_____
Figurative Language	3/4	_____	_____
LANGUAGE	7/10	_____	_____
Complex Sentences			
Compound-Complex Sentences			
Common and Proper Nouns; Abbreviations			
Singular and Plural Nouns			
Possessive Nouns			
TOTAL SCORE	19/26	_____	_____

Were accommodations made in administering this test? ☐ Yes ☐ No

Type of accommodations: _____

_____

COMPREHENSION: Sequential Structure

Directions: Read the passage. Fill in the answer circle in front of the correct answer for each question.

The history of Virginia shows that in 1607, colonists founded Jamestown, the first permanent English settlement in America. More settlers arrived from England and later from Scotland, Ireland, Germany, and elsewhere. In 1619, a governing body called the House of Burgesses met for the first time. In 1693, the College of William and Mary, one of the earliest colleges in the New World, was established.

Virginia is famous as the birthplace of many great leaders, such as George Washington, our first president, who was elected in 1789. In fact, four of our first five presidents were born in Virginia. The others included Thomas Jefferson (the third president), James Madison (the fourth president), and James Monroe (the fifth president). In 1841, two more Virginians became president. William Henry Harrison was elected, but he died after only a month in office. His vice president, John Tyler, took over.

During the Civil War, Virginia sided with the Confederacy. Counties in the western part of Virginia that wanted to remain part of the Union broke away and formed the state of West Virginia. In the course of the war, many fierce battles were fought in Virginia.

Years later, Virginia remains an important state. Other leaders, such as President Woodrow Wilson, were born there. Because part of Virginia is so close to Washington, D.C., many government officials and workers live in Virginia and commute to work. At the beginning of the twenty-first century, Virginia has emerged as a leading state for computer and other high-tech businesses.

Harcourt • Reading and Language Skills Assessment

GO ON

COMPREHENSION: Sequential Structure (continued)

1. How did the author organize the opening paragraph of this passage?
   A He told about events in Virginia's history, using chronological order.
   B He described changes that occurred in Virginia and explained why these changes took place.
   C He gave an opinion about Virginia and supported the opinion with convincing evidence.
   D He told how Virginia is similar to and different from other states.

2. According to the passage, the **first** people to colonize Virginia were from _____.
   A Germany
   B England
   C Scotland
   D Ireland

3. Which happened **first**?
   A George Washington became president.
   B The House of Burgesses met.
   C The College of William and Mary opened.
   D Settlers founded the colony of Jamestown.

4. What happened **soon after** Virginia joined the Confederacy?
   A Many high-tech industries opened in Virginia.
   B West Virginia became a separate state.
   C Government workers moved to Virginia.
   D The Civil War began.

STOP

Score _____

COMPREHENSION: Summarize and Paraphrase

Directions: Read each passage. Fill in the answer circle in front of the correct answer for each question.

Sea otters are among the few animals that use tools. These playful creatures live along the Pacific coast, where they like to eat shellfish and sea urchins. When the animals they want to eat are stuck in cracks in the rocks under the water, sea otters use rocks to tear them loose. To remove the food from its shell, an otter will float on its back with a rock on its chest. Then the otter pounds the shellfish against this hard surface. If that doesn't work, the otter will use another rock as a hammer. Sometimes otters use hard shells, driftwood, or even bottles they have found in the water instead of rocks. If the otter has caught more than one crab or sea urchin, it will wrap the extra ones tightly in seaweed to hold them nearby while it eats.

Otter pups observe their parents using tools, and then they attempt to use tools themselves. They are not always successful. People who study otters have seen pups pounding shellfish against plastic cups and bags that are floating in the water. Sometimes a young otter pretends it has a rock on its chest while it waves its food in the air. If the food is slippery, it can fly out of the otter's paw and back into the water. As they grow up, otters often choose the same kinds of tools that their parents used.

5. Which of these ideas is most important to include in a summary of this passage?
   Ⓐ Sea otters are playful.
   Ⓑ Sea otters use rocks and other objects as tools.
   Ⓒ Slippery food can fly out of a young otter's paw.
   Ⓓ Sometimes the food they want is stuck under the water.

6. What is the best paraphrase of the first sentence of paragraph 2?
   Ⓐ Young otters learn to use tools by watching their parents.
   Ⓑ Otter pups look at their parents' tools, and they also have tools.
   Ⓒ Young otters like to watch their parents.
   Ⓓ Otter pups observe their parents using tools.

GO ON

COMPREHENSION: Summarize and Paraphrase (continued)

Robert the Bruce was a Scottish king. He fought numerous battles, trying to free his people from England's firm grasp. His army had been defeated in five battles. After the fifth defeat, he was forced to hide in a cave to escape from the English.

At this point, Robert the Bruce was discouraged and could see no hope of victory. Then, in the cave in which he was hiding, he saw a spider. The spider was trying to spin a web but was unable to cast its thread to the corner of the wall. Five times the spider tried, and five times it failed.

As he watched, he decided that if the spider was successful, then he would try again to defeat the British. On the sixth try, the spider succeeded.

According to legend, Robert the Bruce was so inspired by the spider's persistence, he vowed to continue his own struggle.

7. Which of the following statements best summarizes this passage?
   Ⓐ Robert the Bruce was a Scottish king who fought numerous battles.
   Ⓑ Robert the Bruce fought five battles against the English and was forced to hide in a cave. In the cave he saw a spider spinning a web. The spider kept trying and trying to spin the web.
   Ⓒ The Scottish king Robert the Bruce, discouraged after being defeated by the British in five battles, was inspired by a spider's persistence to continue his struggle to free his people from England's grasp.
   Ⓓ Robert the Bruce was Scottish. He was discouraged and could see no hope of victory in his battles with the British.

8. What is the best paraphrase of the second sentence of paragraph 1?
   Ⓐ The English had a grip of iron.
   Ⓑ Robert the Bruce fought against British firmness.
   Ⓒ The tight grasp of the British people made him mad.
   Ⓓ He fought many battles as he tried to free his country from English control.

STOP

LITERARY RESPONSE AND ANALYSIS: Point of View

Directions: Read each passage. Fill in the answer circle in front of the correct answer for each question.

The door creaked open slowly. The room was very dark except for a soft glow coming from under a closet door. I opened the closet, shaking with fear about what I might find inside. On a stand inside the closet was a large, lighted aquarium filled with beautiful tropical fish swimming in graceful patterns.

9. Which point of view does the author use to tell this story?
   Ⓐ First person
   Ⓑ Third-person limited
   Ⓒ Third-person omniscient (all-knowing)
   Ⓓ There is not enough evidence in the passage to identify the point of view.

10. Which sentence, if added to the story, would show the same point of view?
   Ⓐ The boy relaxed when he saw the fish.
   Ⓑ I laughed at myself for having been so scared.
   Ⓒ The youngster closed the closet door and left quietly.
   Ⓓ He turned on the light to get a better look at the fish.

GO ON

LITERARY RESPONSE AND ANALYSIS: Point of View (continued)

> The curtain opened, and the school play began. The actors and actresses had been rehearsing for weeks, and the dress rehearsal had gone well. Even so, Justin felt his stomach tighten and beads of sweat pop out on his forehead as he waited for his cue. The cue finally came.

11. Which group of words from the passage shows the third-person limited point of view?

Ⓐ The curtain opened . . .

Ⓑ The school play began.

Ⓒ Justin felt his stomach tighten . . .

Ⓓ The cue finally came.

> It was a miserable day to be outdoors. A cold wind was blowing steadily, and there was a fine mist. Dark clouds were rolling in from the west. The bleachers were barely half-full as the kickoff started the football game.

12. Which sentence, if added to the story, would show the third-person omniscient point of view?

Ⓐ Neither the players nor the fans could concentrate on the game.

Ⓑ Boy, it looks as if we are in for a downpour.

Ⓒ I wonder if the game will be called off due to bad weather.

Ⓓ Before long, we are going to be knee-deep in mud.

STOP

Score _____

Harcourt • Reading and Language Skills Assessment

LITERARY RESPONSE AND ANALYSIS: Figurative Language

Directions: Read the passage. Fill in the answer circle in front of the correct answer for each question.

The human heart is a factory inside your body. When you are born, your heart beats an average of 130 times each minute. As you become an adult, your heart beats about 70 times each minute. Everyone has felt his or her heart pound like a bass drum when exercising or becoming excited. As you relax, your heart returns to normal.

13. Which group of words in this passage is a simile?
   Ⓐ When you are born . . .
   Ⓑ . . .130 times each minute.
   Ⓒ As you become an adult . . .
   Ⓓ . . . heart pound like a bass drum . . .

14. The passage says the human heart is a "factory" because the heart _____.
   Ⓐ is large
   Ⓑ works during the day
   Ⓒ is always working
   Ⓓ makes things

GO ON

LITERARY RESPONSE AND ANALYSIS: Figurative Language (continued)

Directions: Read each sentence. Fill in the answer circle in front of the correct answer for each question.

15. **The cheerful tree waved hello with its leafy arms.**
    This is an example of _____.
    Ⓐ a metaphor
    Ⓑ a simile
    Ⓒ personification
    Ⓓ hyperbole

16. **The athlete's muscles were iron.**
    This is an example of _____.
    Ⓐ a metaphor
    Ⓑ a simile
    Ⓒ personification
    Ⓓ hyperbole

STOP

Score _____
Timeless Treasures / Theme 2

LANGUAGE

Directions: Choose the answer that best describes the underlined words in each sentence.

17. Because a reptile is cold-blooded, its body temperature changes with its surroundings.
   Ⓐ dependent clause
   Ⓑ complex sentence
   Ⓒ compound sentence
   Ⓓ simple sentence

18. As night fell around them, the campers huddled around the campfire; they told scary stories and listened to the sounds of the forest.
   Ⓐ dependent clause
   Ⓑ complex sentence
   Ⓒ compound sentence
   Ⓓ independent clause

19. People on the beach watched with interest as the giant sea turtle moved slowly back toward the water.
   Ⓐ dependent clause
   Ⓑ complex sentence
   Ⓒ subordinating conjunction
   Ⓓ independent clause

Directions: Read the pair of sentences. Choose the answer that shows the best way to combine the sentences to form a complex sentence.

20. The falcon is called a bird of prey. It feeds on other animals.
   Ⓐ The falcon is called a bird; feeds on prey animals.
   Ⓑ The falcon is called a bird, of prey, it feeds on other animals
   Ⓒ The falcon is called a bird of prey because it feeds on other animals.
   Ⓓ Before it feeds, on other animals the falcon is called a bird, of prey.

GO ON

LANGUAGE (continued)

Directions: Read each sentence. Choose the proper noun or abbreviation that should be capitalized in each.

21. Tourists flock to the Smithsonian Institution, a <u>center</u> of <u>learning</u> and <u>research</u> located in Washington, <u>d.c.</u>
    - Ⓐ center
    - Ⓑ learning
    - Ⓒ research
    - Ⓓ d.c.

22. The <u>amazon river</u>, which may have been named by an early Spanish <u>explorer</u>, is 3,900 <u>miles</u> in <u>length</u>.
    - Ⓐ amazon river
    - Ⓑ explorer
    - Ⓒ miles
    - Ⓓ length

Directions: Choose the plural noun that is written correctly.

23. Ⓐ mouses
    Ⓑ beachs
    Ⓒ colonies
    Ⓓ lifes

24. Ⓐ doctores
    Ⓑ teeth
    Ⓒ heros
    Ⓓ communityes

GO ON

Timeless Treasures / Theme 2

Harcourt • Reading and Language Skills Assessment

LANGUAGE (continued)

Directions: Choose the correct possessive noun to complete each sentence.

25. The _____ volleyball team at our school won first place in the tournament.
Ⓐ girls'
Ⓑ girls
Ⓒ girls's
Ⓓ girl

26. The _____ clothes were covered with muddy pawprints.
Ⓐ childrens
Ⓑ children's
Ⓒ childrens'
Ⓓ childrens's

STOP

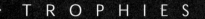

Friends to the Rescue / Theme 2
Reading and Language Skills Assessment

Harcourt

Orlando   Boston   Dallas   Chicago   San Diego

Part No. 9997-37772-9

ISBN 0-15-332212-8 (Package of 12)

6

· T R O P H I E S ·

Reading and Language Skills
Assessment Pretest

Timeless Treasures / Theme 3

Name _____ Date _____

SKILL AREA	Criterion Score	Pupil Score	Pupil Strength
COMPREHENSION			
Text Structure: Main Idea and Details	3/4	_____	_____
RESEARCH AND INFORMATION SKILLS			
Locate Information	3/4	_____	_____
Graphic Aids	3/4	_____	_____
LANGUAGE	7/10	_____	_____
Subject and Object Pronouns Case; Possessive Pronouns Reflexive Pronouns and Indefinite Pronouns Adjectives and Articles Proper and Demonstrative Adjectives			
TOTAL SCORE	16/22	_____	_____

Were accommodations made in administering this test? ❏ Yes ❏ No

Type of accommodations: _____

_____

ISBN 0-15-332212-8

3 4 5 6 7 8 9 10   170   10 09 08 07 06 05 04 03 02

COMPREHENSION: Text Structure: Main Idea and Details

Directions: Read the passage. Fill in the answer circle in front of the correct answer for each question.

Even though deserts have little water and high temperatures, many animals have learned to survive there. In the daytime, few of these creatures are active. But as the sun begins to go down, more and more animals emerge to look for food.

The most common desert animals are insects, which usually feed on plants. Many other animals eat plants as well, including camels and antelope. Rodents often eat seeds that they find on the ground. Some rodents, like kangaroo rats, gather up food when they can find it and hide it for later. Some reptiles also store food, but they store it as fat in their tails.

There are birds in the desert, too. Most of them are insect-eaters, although some eat seeds or fruit. Unlike other desert creatures, birds must be able to fly to a water source. Except for owls and a few other birds of the night, most birds look for food in the early morning or in the evening.

Camels are probably the best-known desert animals. They can go for several days without drinking water. They do not store water in their humps, however. Instead, they use the fat stored there for energy. When they do find water, they can drink a lot of it very quickly.

GO ON

COMPREHENSION: Text Structure: Main Idea and Details (continued)

1. What is the main idea of this passage?
   - (A) Deserts have high temperatures.
   - (B) Camels are well-known desert animals.
   - (C) In spite of harsh conditions, many animals live in deserts.
   - (D) The most common animals found in deserts are insects.

2. Which detail would best support the main idea?
   - (A) Even cold-blooded animals, such as snakes, generally avoid the direct heat of the desert sun.
   - (B) Guinea pigs, gerbils, squirrels, chipmunks, mice, and rats are also members of the rodent family.
   - (C) Marco Polo is said to have ridden on a camel during his travels from Europe to Asia.
   - (D) Birds are found in just about every habitat on Earth, including the polar regions.

3. Which detail could best be added to this passage?
   - (A) Big Bend National Park in Texas has desert areas.
   - (B) Desert rabbits have large ears, which let heat escape.
   - (C) Phoenix, Arizona, is a large city with a desert climate.
   - (D) A cactus stores water in its stem and leaves.

4. Which detail could best be added to paragraph 3?
   - (A) Bats are mammals.
   - (B) The ostrich and penguin are birds that cannot fly.
   - (C) Vultures are well-known desert birds that eat dead animals.
   - (D) Many lizards live in the desert and eat insects.

STOP

Score _____

Harcourt • Reading and Language Skills Assessment

RESEARCH AND INFORMATION SKILLS: Locate Information

Directions: Study the index shown below. Then fill in the answer circle in front of the correct answer for each question.

Index

Active solar heating, *E72*
Adirondack Mountains, *E76*
African elephant, *B83*
Air, and sound, *C55, C57*
Air roots, *F84*
Alexander the Great, *D26*
Allen, Glenn, *B88*
Alligator, *B79*
Alps Mountains, *A42*

5. Where would be the **best** place to look to read about solar panels?
- Ⓐ E72
- Ⓑ B83
- Ⓒ B88
- Ⓓ A42

6. On which **two** pages could you read about mountains?
- Ⓐ E76 and C55
- Ⓑ C55 and C57
- Ⓒ E76 and A42
- Ⓓ B79 and A42

GO ON

RESEARCH AND INFORMATION SKILLS: Locate Information (continued)

Directions: Study the index shown below. Then fill in the answer circle in front of the correct answer for each question.

INDEX

Births	2B	Classifieds	5D	Movies	9E	StateNews	1A
Business	6C	Comics	11E	Puzzles	12E	Weather	7D
City Life	8E	Editorials	3B	Sports	4D	TV Listings	10E

7. Which page would list the times that TV shows will be on?

Ⓐ 1A

Ⓑ 8E

Ⓒ 10E

Ⓓ 11E

8. Which of the following are you **most likely** to find on page 1A?

Ⓐ a review of a new movie

Ⓑ a report on the governor's speech

Ⓒ the results of last night's local football games

Ⓓ a listing of births at local hospitals

STOP

Harcourt • Reading and Language Skills Assessment

RESEARCH AND INFORMATION SKILLS: Graphic Aids

Directions: Study the two circle graphs below. Then fill in the answer circle in front of the correct answer for each question.

Ray's Monthly Expenses

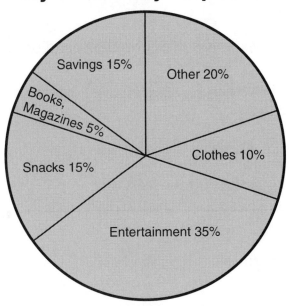

Carmen's Monthly Expenses

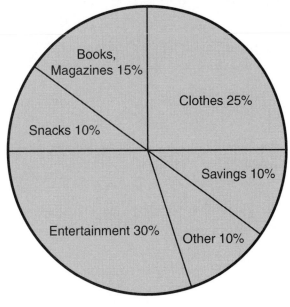

GO ON

RESEARCH AND INFORMATION SKILLS: Graphic Aids (continued)

9. What percent of his expenses does Ray spend on snacks?

(A) 15%

(B) 20%

(C) 30%

(D) 35%

10. What percent of her expenses does Carmen spend on savings?

(A) 5%

(B) 10%

(C) 15%

(D) 20%

11. What expense does Ray spend the least on?

(A) Savings

(B) Snacks

(C) Books and Magazines

(D) Other

12. What expense do both Carmen and Ray spend the most on?

(A) Snacks

(B) Clothes

(C) Entertainment

(D) Books and Magazines

STOP

Score _____

LANGUAGE

Directions: Choose the answer that best describes the underlined word in each sentence.

13. Are <u>we</u> allowed to take pictures inside the natural history museum?
    - Ⓐ subject pronoun; singular
    - Ⓑ subject pronoun; plural
    - Ⓒ object pronoun; singular
    - Ⓓ object pronoun; plural

14. The children's grandparents bought <u>them</u> in-line skates, pads, and helmets.
    - Ⓐ subject pronoun; singular
    - Ⓑ subject pronoun; plural
    - Ⓒ object pronoun; singular
    - Ⓓ object pronoun; plural

Directions: Choose the answer that gives the antecedent of the underlined pronoun in the sentence.

15. Bob finished his math homework, so he closed his book and put <u>it</u> in his backpack.
    - Ⓐ Bob
    - Ⓑ closed
    - Ⓒ book
    - Ⓓ backpack

16. The mayor tried <u>his</u> best to convince the people attending the rally to vote in the election for city council.
    - Ⓐ mayor
    - Ⓑ people
    - Ⓒ rally
    - Ⓓ council

GO ON

LANGUAGE (continued)

Directions: Choose the pronoun that correctly completes each sentence.

17. Manuel's father took _____ on a weekend camping trip in the mountains.
    - (A) his
    - (B) him
    - (C) himself
    - (D) he

18. Marissa and Eric were surprised that they were able to move the heavy box all by _____ .
    - (A) their
    - (B) they
    - (C) theirs
    - (D) themselves

Directions: Choose the underlined word in each sentence that is an **adjective**.

19. The <u>delegates</u> to the United Nations listened as the <u>ambassador</u> gave a <u>fiery</u> <u>speech</u>.
    - (A) delegates
    - (B) ambassador
    - (C) fiery
    - (D) speech

20. The <u>scientists</u> found <u>these</u> <u>pieces</u> of pottery as <u>they</u> explored the cave.
    - (A) scientists
    - (B) these
    - (C) pieces
    - (D) they

GO ON

LANGUAGE (continued)

Directions: Choose the **adjective** that should be capitalized in each sentence.

21. In A.D. 43, the <u>mighty</u> emperor Claudius conquered the <u>cold</u>, <u>misty</u> island of Britain, which remained a <u>roman</u> province for nearly 400 years.

Ⓐ mighty

Ⓑ cold

Ⓒ misty

Ⓓ roman

22. My mother is a <u>great</u> cook who enjoys making <u>mexican</u> dishes, such as <u>tasty</u> chicken enchiladas covered with <u>white</u> cheese.

Ⓐ great

Ⓑ mexican

Ⓒ tasty

Ⓓ white

STOP

Unlocking the Past / Theme 3
Reading and Language Skills Assessment

Harcourt

Orlando   Boston   Dallas   Chicago   San Diego

Part No. 9997-37779-6

ISBN 0-15-332212-8 (Package of 12)

6

Reading and Language Skills Assessment Posttest

Timeless Treasures / Theme 3

Name _____ Date _____

SKILL AREA	Criterion Score	Pupil Score	Pupil Strength
COMPREHENSION Text Structure: Main Idea and Details	3/4	_____	_____
RESEARCH AND INFORMATION SKILLS Locate Information Graphic Aids	3/4 3/4	_____ _____	_____ _____
LANGUAGE Subject and Object Pronouns Case; Possessive Pronouns Reflexive Pronouns and Indefinite Pronouns Adjectives and Articles Proper and Demonstrative Adjectives	7/10	_____	_____
TOTAL SCORE	16/22	_____	_____

Were accommodations made in administering this test? ☐ Yes ☐ No

Type of accommodations: _____

_____

Printed in the United States of America

ISBN 0-15-332212-8

3 4 5 6 7 8 9 10   170   10 09 08 07 06 05 04 03 02

COMPREHENSION: Text Structure: Main Idea and Details

Directions: Read the passage. Fill in the answer circle in front of the correct answer for each question.

Liechtenstein is one of the smallest countries in the world. It is located in Europe between Austria and Switzerland. The entire country has a land area of only 62 square miles! The population is just over 30,000 citizens. The official state language is German, but many people speak other languages as well.

The economy of Liechtenstein has changed dramatically in the last forty years. In the 1960s, it was based largely on agriculture. Today it is based on industry, banking, and tourism. There are few farmers left. Factories in Liechtenstein produce machinery, medicines, and other products. People there use Swiss francs for money.

The country is known for its low taxes. For that reason many corporations have their home offices there. Liechtenstein has also been known for finely engraved postage stamps.

Politically, Liechtenstein is closely allied with Switzerland. It has a constitution, but it also has a ruling family. Women did not receive the right to vote in national elections there until 1984. On the other hand, the country has not had an army since 1868.

GO ON

Harcourt • Reading and Language Skills Assessment

COMPREHENSION: Text Structure: Main Idea and Details (continued)

1. What is the main idea of this passage?
   - (A) The economy of Liechtenstein has changed.
   - (B) Liechtenstein is closely allied with Switzerland.
   - (C) Women in Liechtenstein could not vote until 1984.
   - (D) Liechtenstein is a small but interesting country.

2. Which detail would best support the main idea?
   - (A) Liechtenstein has a prince who appoints a chief of government.
   - (B) Many people in Switzerland speak two or three languages.
   - (C) There is a mountain range called the Alps in Europe.
   - (D) Both World War I and II were fought in Europe.

3. Which detail could best be added to this passage?
   - (A) Agricultural businesses include dairy farms.
   - (B) Liechtenstein joined the United Nations in 1990.
   - (C) The Cayman Islands also have liberal tax laws.
   - (D) The Hapsburg family ruled Austria until Word War I.

4. Which detail could best be added to paragraph 3?
   - (A) The stamps are copies of paintings owned by the ruling family.
   - (B) The modern history of the country began in 1719.
   - (C) Prince Hans Adam came to power in 1989.
   - (D) There are 25 members in the country's parliament.

STOP

Score _____

RESEARCH AND INFORMATION SKILLS: Locate Information

Directions: Study the index shown below. Then fill in the answer circle in front of the correct answer for each question.

Section .... Page	
Announcements 8B	
Arts 9E	
Births 11B	
Business 2F	
Classifieds 12C	
Comics 10E	
Headlines 1A	
Movies 6E	
Personals 13B	
Real Estate 3D	
Sports 4G	
Television 7E	
Weather 5G	

5. What page would tell you if rain is predicted for this weekend?
   - Ⓐ 1A
   - Ⓑ 5G
   - Ⓒ 6E
   - Ⓓ 7E

6. In which section are you **most likely** to find an article about a new play?
   - Ⓐ Business
   - Ⓑ Television
   - Ⓒ Classifieds
   - Ⓓ Arts

GO ON

RESEARCH AND INFORMATION SKILLS: Locate Information (continued)

Directions: Study the Table of Contents shown below. Then fill in the answer circle in front of the correct answer for each question.

7. To find out about industries that have been important in America, the **best** place to look would be on page _____.

   (A) 483

   (B) 509

   (C) 518

   (D) 532

8. Which of these is most likely found on **page 525**?

   (A) a map of important cattle ranches

   (B) a map of California showing mining locations

   (C) a line graph showing the growth of cities

   (D) a table showing numbers of immigrants

STOP

Score _____

Harcourt • Reading and Language Skills Assessment

RESEARCH AND INFORMATION SKILLS: Graphic Aids

Directions: Study the bar graph and chart shown below. Fill in the answer circle in front of the correct answer for each question.

Chart of Animal Speeds	
Cheetah	70
Chicken	9
Elephant	25
Giraffe	32
Human	27.89
Lion	50
Quarter Horse	47.5

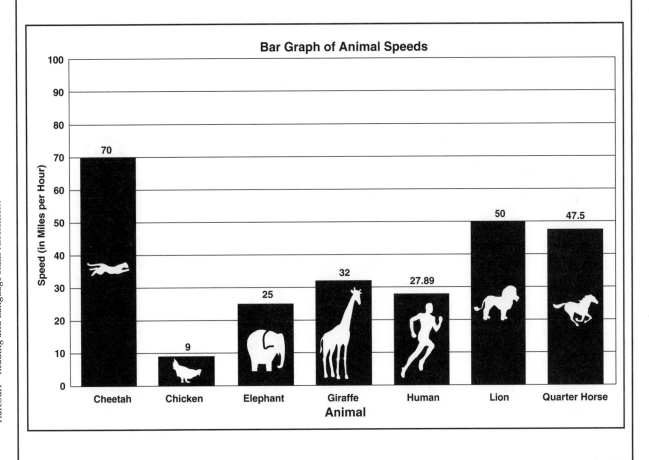

GO ON

RESEARCH AND INFORMATION SKILLS: Graphic Aids (continued)

9. Which animal is the fastest?
   Ⓐ cheetah
   Ⓑ chicken
   Ⓒ elephant
   Ⓓ giraffe

10. How many miles per hour can the giraffe travel?
    Ⓐ 9
    Ⓑ 25
    Ⓒ 32
    Ⓓ 70

11. Which animal listed is slower than a human?
    Ⓐ elephant
    Ⓑ giraffe
    Ⓒ lion
    Ⓓ quarter horse

12. According to the information given, how many miles per hour can the fastest animal run?
    Ⓐ 50
    Ⓑ 70
    Ⓒ 80
    Ⓓ 100

STOP

Score _____

LANGUAGE

Directions: Choose the answer that best describes the underlined words in each sentence.

13. Animals and plants have adaptations that allow <u>them</u> to survive in their habitats.

    Ⓐ subject pronoun; singular

    Ⓑ subject pronoun; plural

    Ⓒ object pronoun; singular

    Ⓓ object pronoun; plural

14. I see Hector only on weekends because <u>he</u> goes to a private school.

    Ⓐ subject pronoun; singular

    Ⓑ subject pronoun; plural

    Ⓒ object pronoun; singular

    Ⓓ object pronoun; plural

Directions: Choose the answer that gives the **antecedent** of the underlined pronoun in the sentence.

15. People help conserve energy when <u>they</u> carpool or ride the bus to work.

    Ⓐ People

    Ⓑ energy

    Ⓒ bus

    Ⓓ work

16. As towns and cities grow larger, animals often lose <u>their</u> homes.

    Ⓐ towns

    Ⓑ cities

    Ⓒ grow

    Ⓓ animals

GO ON

LANGUAGE (continued)

Directions: Choose the pronoun that correctly completes each sentence.

17. When my family visited Boston last year, _____ toured Paul Revere's house.
    - (A) us
    - (B) ours
    - (C) we
    - (D) ourselves

18. The table was covered with desserts, so my cousins and I helped _____ to cookies and ice cream.
    - (A) ours
    - (B) ourselves
    - (C) us
    - (D) we

Directions: Choose the underlined word in each sentence that is an **adjective**.

19. That store on the corner is where my brother bought his CD player.
    - (A) That
    - (B) store
    - (C) corner
    - (D) player

20. The queen's crown contained an enormous diamond that sparkled like a star.
    - (A) crown
    - (B) enormous
    - (C) sparkled
    - (D) star

GO ON ▶

Harcourt • Reading and Language Skills Assessment

LANGUAGE (continued)

Directions: Choose the **adjective** that should be capitalized in each sentence.

21. The sunny and wealthy state of California was named by spanish explorers who sailed along its beautiful coast.

Ⓐ sunny

Ⓑ wealthy

Ⓒ spanish

Ⓓ beautiful

22. Visitors to the south american country of Brazil find many interesting attractions, such as cities with richly decorated buildings built during colonial days.

Ⓐ south american

Ⓑ interesting

Ⓒ decorated

Ⓓ days

STOP

• T R O P H I E S •

Unlocking the Past / Theme 3
Reading and Language Skills Assessment

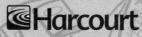

Harcourt

Orlando   Boston   Dallas   Chicago   San Diego

Part No. 9997-37773-7

ISBN 0-15-332212-8 (Package of 12)

6

TROPHIES

Mid-Year Reading and Language Skills Assessment

Timeless Treasures / Themes 1, 2, 3

Name_____ Date_____

SKILL AREA	Criterion Score	Pupil Score	Pupil Strength
VOCABULARY AND CONCEPTS	3/4	_____	_____
COMPREHENSION	7/10	_____	_____
LITERARY RESPONSE AND ANALYSIS	6/8	_____	_____
RESEARCH AND INFORMATION SKILLS	4/6	_____	_____
LANGUAGE	9/12	_____	_____
TOTAL SCORE	29/40	_____	_____

Were accommodations made in administering this test? ❑ Yes ❑ No

Type of accommodations: _____

Comments _____

_____

_____

VOCABULARY AND CONCEPTS

Directions: Fill in the answer circle in front of the correct answer for each question.

1. Which prefix should be added to the word *bitter* to make it mean "to cause someone to feel bitter"?

   Ⓐ *un-*

   Ⓑ *em-*

   Ⓒ *non-*

   Ⓓ *pre-*

2. Which suffix should be added to the word *swamp* to make it mean "consisting of swamps"?

   Ⓐ *-ment*

   Ⓑ *-ful*

   Ⓒ *-y*

   Ⓓ *-ial*

3. **I wish my brother wouldn't always interrupt me.**
   What does the root "rupt" mean?

   Ⓐ between

   Ⓑ voice

   Ⓒ time

   Ⓓ break

4. Which root word means *speak*?

   Ⓐ "dict" as in **dictate**

   Ⓑ "miss" as in **mission**

   Ⓒ "graph" as in **photograph**

   Ⓓ "vis" as in **vision**

COMPREHENSION

Directions: Read each passage. Fill in the answer circle in front of the correct answer for each question.

The mystery of Amelia Earhart has fascinated people since her disappearance in 1937. Amelia Earhart was born in Atchison, Kansas, in 1897. She worked as a military nurse and as a social worker. What she really wanted to do was fly, but her family did not approve. In 1920, though, she learned to fly a plane.

Soon, Amelia Earhart began setting records. In 1928, she became the first woman to fly across the Atlantic Ocean. Earhart was only a passenger on that flight. In 1932, she flew alone from Newfoundland to Ireland in a record time of 14 hours 56 minutes. She wrote about her adventures in a book titled *The Fun of It.* Then she made an even longer trip from Hawaii to California. In 1935, she became the first person to travel that route successfully.

As she set records, Earhart also helped the new airline business by encouraging the development of airplanes. Her final adventure, however, ended in tragedy. In 1937, Earhart set out to fly around the world. Her plane disappeared near Howland Island in the Pacific Ocean, and she was never heard from again.

5. How did the author organize the second paragraph of this passage?
   - Ⓐ He compared Amelia Earhart's skill as a pilot with that of other pilots of the period.
   - Ⓑ He told about Amelia Earhart's flights, using chronological order.
   - Ⓒ He described problems Earhart faced while flying and told how she solved them.
   - Ⓓ He described a change in Amelia Earhart's attitude about flying and explained why this change took place.

6. Which of these happened **after** Amelia Earhart successfully flew from Hawaii to California?
   - Ⓐ She wrote a book titled *The Fun of it.*
   - Ⓑ She became the first woman to fly across the Atlantic Ocean.
   - Ⓒ She set out to fly around the world.
   - Ⓓ She worked as a military nurse.

COMPREHENSION (continued)

Every October, thousands of athletes from around the world travel to Hawaii for a special sports event—the Ironman Triathlon World Championship. These people have spent months and years training. To qualify for the Ironman Triathlon, they must have successfully completed a local triathlon.

At 7 A.M. two thousand people jump into Kailua Bay and start swimming. They swim as fast as they can in the choppy ocean for 2.4 miles. But the race isn't over yet. The athletes exit the water and quickly dry off. Then they put on clothing and shoes and leap onto their bicycles. They race 112 miles over the hills and into the beautiful Hawaiian valleys. When they finish the bicycle race, they change into running clothes and shoes and start running. The 26.2-mile marathon is the last part of this amazing event. Not everybody makes it. Some are too tired, and others are injured along the way.

It takes the winners more than eight hours to finish the course. As the athletes cross the finish line, they are each given a Hawaiian necklace of flowers called a "lei."

7. In the second paragraph of this passage, the author _____.

Ⓐ gives an opinion about triathlons and offers convincing evidence

Ⓑ describes differences and similarities between old and young athletes

Ⓒ describes the different segments of the triathlon in the order in which they occur

Ⓓ tells about problems that occur during a triathlon and gives solutions for the problems

8. What do the athletes do **last** in the triathlon?

Ⓐ swim

Ⓑ skate

Ⓒ bicycle

Ⓓ run

COMPREHENSION (continued)

Yo-yos have a long and fascinating history. They are considered the second-oldest toy, with the doll being the oldest. Although we do not know exactly when yo-yos came into existence, we do know that they were used in Greece between 400 and 500 B.C. Examples of yo-yos from that period can be found in the Metropolitan Museum of Art. Grecian urns from that time have drawings showing yo-yo tricks.

Yo-yos were used in the Philippines hundreds of years ago, first as a weapon rather than a toy. Filipinos used them to stun prey. They hunted animals by dropping the heavy wooden disks from tree branches. When they missed, the attached strings allowed them to retrieve the disks so that they could try again. Later, yo-yos came into use there as toys. Filipinos became expert players, playing from childhood into their adult years. In fact, the word *yo-yo* is said to have come from Tagalog, the native language of the Philippines. It means "come back."

Yo-yos were also popular in the 1700s and 1800s in France. Napoleon was known to have carried and used a yo-yo during that time. Furthermore, a picture painted in 1789 shows King Louis XVII using a yo-yo. That painting hangs today in the Louvre museum in Paris, France.

People in the United States started playing with the British "bandalore," another name for the yo-yo, in the 1860s; but it was not until the 1920s that a Filipino named Pedro Flores began manufacturing a toy labeled "yo-yo." Working out of a small toy factory in California, Flores was the first person to mass-produce yo-yos.

It is said that D. F. Duncan, a famous inventor and savvy marketer, saw a young man playing with one of Flores's yo-yos in 1927 and realized the marketing potential of the toy. Duncan worked out a deal with newspaper tycoon W. R. Hearst to advertise the toys. A couple of years later, in 1929, Duncan bought the rights from Flores and started the Genuine Duncan Yo-Yo company. He trademarked the name yo-yo. Although he did not invent the yo-yo, he is responsible for the first yo-yo fad in the United States.

Harcourt • Reading and Language Skills Assessment

COMPREHENSION (continued)

9. What is the main idea of this passage?

Ⓐ Yo-yos have a long and fascinating history.

Ⓑ Yo-yos were first used in the Philippines hundreds of years ago.

Ⓒ Pedro Flores was the first person to mass-produce yo-yos.

Ⓓ D.F. Duncan worked out a deal with W. R. Hearst to advertise yo-yos.

10. Which detail could best be added to this passage?

Ⓐ The Metropolitan Museum of Art is located in New York.

Ⓑ The first patent for a yo-yo in the United States was issued in 1866.

Ⓒ The Philippine Islands once belonged to Spain.

Ⓓ D. F. Duncan originated the idea of sending in cereal box tops to get a free prize.

11. Yo-yos were first mass-produced in _____.

Ⓐ Greece

Ⓑ France

Ⓒ the Philippines

Ⓓ the United States

12. Which language did the word *yo-yo* probably come from?

Ⓐ English

Ⓑ Greek

Ⓒ Tagalog

Ⓓ French

COMPREHENSION (continued)

The modern calendar is based on the period of time needed for the earth to orbit the sun. The ancient Egyptians had the first calendar based on the sun. Their year began when the brightest star rose in the same place that the sun rose. The Egyptians figured out that a year was 365 days long. However, their calendar had a problem that made it somewhat inaccurate. A year is actually about one-quarter of a day longer than 365 days. After a while, the Egyptian calendar no longer matched the seasons.

Julius Caesar, dictator of ancient Rome, corrected the problem of the extra quarter-day by adding a day at the end of February every four years. In 1582 the calendar was changed again, this time by Pope Gregory XIII. His calendar was very similar to the one we use today.

13. What is the best summary of this passage?

(A) The modern calendar is based on the sun, as was a calendar used by the ancient Egyptians. Their calendar had a problem involving the number of days in a year. This problem was corrected by Julius Caesar. Pope Gregory XIII made additional changes, producing a calendar that is very similar to the one we use today.

(B) Our calendar is based on the earth's orbit around the sun, and the ancient Egyptians had the first calendar in which the year began when the brightest star rose in the same place. A year is actually about one-quarter of a day longer.

(C) Our calendar is like the ancient Egyptians' calendar, but their calendar was somewhat inaccurate; after a while, the Egyptian calendar no longer matched the seasons.

(D) The Egyptians figured out that a year was 365 days long, but their calendar had a problem. Julius Caesar, dictator of ancient Rome, corrected the problem.

14. What is the best paraphrase of the first sentence of this passage?

(A) The calendar is based on the earth and the sun.

(B) Our calendar is based on the time it takes the earth to travel around the sun.

(C) Today's calendar is based on time and the sun.

(D) The calendar we use today has to do with the sun moving around the earth.

Harcourt • Reading and Language Skills Assessment

Score _____

LITERARY RESPONSE AND ANALYSIS

Directions: Read each passage. Fill in the answer circle in front of the correct answer for each question.

"Mom!" Allie screeched at the top of her lungs. "She's done it again!"

"What's the matter, Allie?" her mother asked as she walked into Allie's bedroom.

"Jennifer, that's what's the matter! I just started to get out my red sweater to wear to school today. It wasn't in the drawer where I know I put it last, it wasn't in the closet, and I just found it—wadded up in a ball on the floor by Jennifer's bed. It's a wrinkled mess. I don't want her wearing my clothes or borrowing anything from me anymore. She treats my stuff like garbage. She breaks things, she never puts anything back where she got it, and she's just awful! You've got to do something, Mom."

"I'm sorry about your sweater, Allie. Just try to figure out something else to wear today. I'll have a talk with Jennifer. I don't blame you for being angry."

Mom went down the hall to locate Jennifer. She found her eating a piece of toast in the kitchen.

"Good morning, Mom," Jennifer smiled.

Mom responded, "It was a good morning until Allie found her favorite red sweater crumpled on the floor where you left it. Honestly, Jennifer, I don't know how you can be so inconsiderate about other people's things. It's time for you to go to school now, but after supper tonight, we're going to have a family meeting. I am not pleased with your behavior."

Jennifer didn't say anything back. She hung her head guiltily, grabbed her books, and went out to meet the school bus.

That night after a quiet dinner together, Mom, Jennifer, and Allie sat down in the living room. Mom delivered her expected lecture on how important it is to respect other people's property. She was prepared to quickly interrupt any harsh statements the sisters started to make to each other. To her surprise, though, there were no fireworks.

Jennifer said, "I've already apologized to Allie, Mom. We ate together in the cafeteria today and talked about all this. I don't mean to mess up her stuff or break it or leave it lying around. I just do things without thinking sometimes. I've promised Allie that I'll try to be more thoughtful and treat her things with more respect from now on. She says she'll let me keep borrowing stuff from her—on a trial basis. I'll try not to let you down."

LITERARY RESPONSE AND ANALYSIS (continued)

15. When does this story take place?
    Ⓐ on a weekend
    Ⓑ during the summer
    Ⓒ on a school day
    Ⓓ on a holiday

16. Based on her actions at the beginning of the story, Jennifer could best be described as _____.
    Ⓐ patient
    Ⓑ nervous
    Ⓒ generous
    Ⓓ inconsiderate

17. What is the main problem in this story?
    Ⓐ Jennifer does not treat her sister's belongings with respect.
    Ⓑ Allie is jealous of all the attention Jennifer gets from Mom.
    Ⓒ Jennifer and Allie are not keeping up with their schoolwork.
    Ⓓ Allie and Jennifer don't help Mom enough with housework.

18. How is the problem solved?
    Ⓐ Mom decides to spend private time with Allie on weekends.
    Ⓑ Jennifer agrees to try to change her behavior.
    Ⓒ The girls plan to do their homework together in the evenings.
    Ⓓ Mom assigns certain chores for Jennifer and Allie to do.

Harcourt • Reading and Language Skills Assessment

LITERARY RESPONSE AND ANALYSIS (continued)

> The voyage to the space station was the first time Dan or Anna had been away from Earth in quite a while. The blastoff, the journey, and the docking all went smoothly. The station itself was comfortable and well stocked with supplies. Dan, Anna, and the other crew members were confident that the mission would be a success. Little did they know of the terrible problems that awaited them.

19. Which point of view does the author use to tell this story?

Ⓐ First person

Ⓑ Third-person limited (to Dan's view)

Ⓒ Third-person omniscient (all-knowing)

Ⓓ There is not enough evidence in the passage to identify the point of view.

20. Which sentence, if added to the story, would show the same point of view?

Ⓐ Lurking in the storage compartment was an unexpected visitor.

Ⓑ I paid close attention to every detail about the station's operation.

Ⓒ Most members of my crew had little experience in space.

Ⓓ We looked out the window at Earth, a small greenish-blue dot.

LITERARY RESPONSE AND ANALYSIS (continued)

The carefree locomotive hummed and whistled as it made its way through the rolling countryside. The passengers gazed out the windows, admiring the beautiful landscape that was as green as an emerald. The ground was still wet with dew that reflected the early morning sunlight. Fat cattle grazed, undisturbed by the passing train. The train track curved around a large lake, quiet except for the occasional ripple caused by birds diving for food.

21. Which group of words in this passage is a simile?

(A) . . . through the rolling countryside.

(B) landscape . . . was as green as an emerald.

(C) Fat cattle grazed . . .

(D) The train track curved . . .

22. Which group of words in this passage is an example of personification?

(A) The carefree locomotive hummed and whistled . . .

(B) . . . gazed out the windows . . .

(C) . . . wet with dew . . .

(D) . . . birds diving for food.

Score _____

Timeless Treasures / Mid-Year Skills

RESEARCH AND INFORMATION SKILLS

Directions: Study the Table of Contents shown below. Then fill in the answer circle in front of the correct answer for each question.

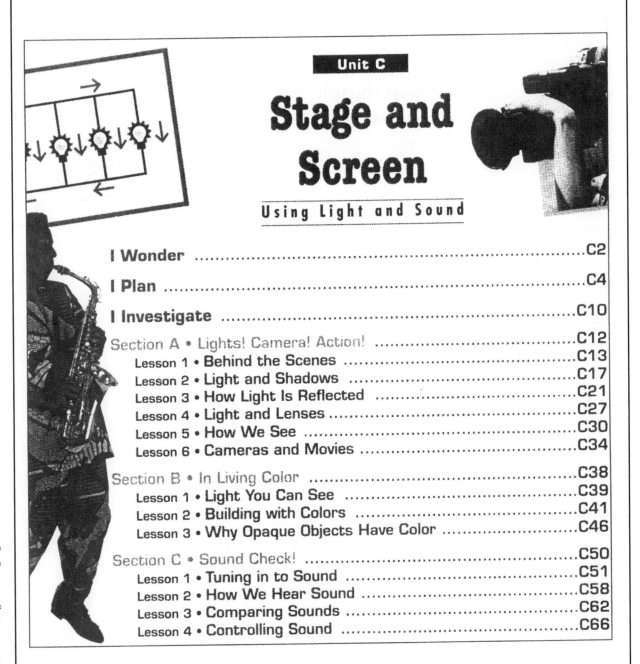

Unit C

Stage and Screen

Using Light and Sound

RESEARCH AND INFORMATION SKILLS (continued)

23. To find out why objects have different colors, the **best** place to look would be in _____.

Ⓐ Section A, Lesson 2

Ⓑ Section A, Lesson 6

Ⓒ Section B, Lesson 3

Ⓓ Section C, Lesson 3

24. Which choice would **most likely** be found on page **C30**?

Ⓐ an article about how loud sounds can be harmful

Ⓑ a list of different sounds

Ⓒ a chart of colors

Ⓓ a diagram of the eye

Harcourt • Reading and Language Skills Assessment

RESEARCH AND INFORMATION SKILLS (continued)

Directions: Study the line graph and diagram shown below. Fill in the answer circle in front of the correct answer for each question.

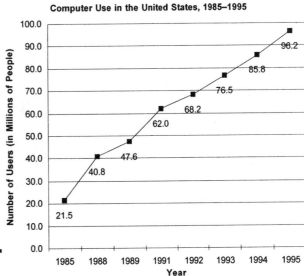

Computer Use in the United States, 1985–1995

Number of Users (in Millions of People)

96.2
85.8
76.5
68.2
62.0
47.6
40.8
21.5

Year: 1985 1988 1989 1991 1992 1993 1994 1995

Diagram of a Computer

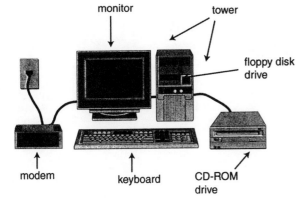

monitor
tower
floppy disk drive
modem
keyboard
CD-ROM drive

RESEARCH AND INFORMATION SKILLS (continued)

25. According to the information given, which of the following is **not** a part of a computer?

Ⓐ modem   Ⓑ handset

Ⓒ keyboard   Ⓓ monitor

26. Which of these years is **not** included in the line graph?

Ⓐ 1988   Ⓑ 1989

Ⓒ 1990   Ⓓ 1991

27. What was the greatest number of computer users during the years 1988 to 1993?

Ⓐ 100 million   Ⓑ 96.2 million

Ⓒ 76.5 million   Ⓓ 40.8 million

28. According to the diagram, which part of a computer contains the floppy disk drive?

Ⓐ modem   Ⓑ CD-ROM drive

Ⓒ keyboard   Ⓓ tower

LANGUAGE

Directions: Choose the best answer for each question.

29. Choose the underlined noun that is the **simple subject** of this sentence.

The skilled potter fashioned the lump of clay into an oval-shaped bowl.

Ⓐ potter

Ⓑ lump

Ⓒ clay

Ⓓ bowl

30. Choose the answer that best describes the underlined words in this sentence.

By the time Martin Luther King, Jr., died in 1968, his words had done much to stir the nation, and he continues to be honored as a champion of civil rights.

Ⓐ independent clause

Ⓑ complex sentence

Ⓒ compound sentence

Ⓓ dependent clause

Directions: Read each pair of sentences. Choose the answer that shows the best way to combine the sentences.

31. An ostrich cannot fly. It can run at speeds up to 40 miles per hour.

Ⓐ An ostrich cannot fly; run at speeds up to 40 miles per hour.

Ⓑ An ostrich cannot fly, or it can run at speeds up to 40 miles per hour.

Ⓒ An ostrich cannot fly, but it can run at speeds up to 40 miles per hour.

Ⓓ An ostrich cannot fly and it can run at speeds up to 40 miles per hour.

LANGUAGE (continued)

32. People believe that a camel's hump stores water. It actually stores fat.

    Ⓐ Before a camel stores fat people believe it stores water.

    Ⓑ Although people believe that a camel's hump stores water, it actually stores fat.

    Ⓒ Because people believe that a camel's hump stores water, it actually stores fat.

    Ⓓ If people believe that a camel's hump stores water it actually stores fat.

Directions: Choose the plural noun that is written correctly.

33. Ⓐ trouts

    Ⓑ factorys

    Ⓒ curtaines

    Ⓓ grasses

34. Ⓐ quiltes

    Ⓑ leaves

    Ⓒ wifes

    Ⓓ childs

Directions: Choose the correct possessive noun to complete each sentence.

35. The _____ musical club meets every Thursday afternoon.

    Ⓐ women's

    Ⓑ women

    Ⓒ womens'

    Ⓓ womens's

36. The _____ engine was damaged by the freezing temperatures.

    Ⓐ cars's

    Ⓑ cars

    Ⓒ car's

    Ⓓ cars'

LANGUAGE (continued)

Directions: Choose the pronoun that correctly completes each sentence.

37. Rosa's science project is about animals and their habitats, but _____ is about chemical reactions.

Ⓐ my

Ⓑ mine

Ⓒ myself

Ⓓ I

38. The marathon runners keep _____ bodies in shape by running several miles each day.

Ⓐ theirs

Ⓑ they

Ⓒ their

Ⓓ them

Directions: Choose the underlined word in each sentence that is an **adjective.**

39. The <u>ancient</u> <u>Greeks</u> built the <u>city</u> of Athens around a <u>hill</u> called the Acropolis.

Ⓐ ancient

Ⓑ Greeks

Ⓒ city

Ⓓ hill

40. I found <u>these</u> arrowheads in a <u>cave</u> I <u>explored</u> with a <u>friend</u>.

Ⓐ these

Ⓑ cave

Ⓒ explored

Ⓓ friend

STOP

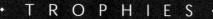

Timeless Treasures / Themes 1, 2, 3
Mid-Year Reading and Language Skills Assessment

Harcourt

Orlando Boston Dallas Chicago San Diego

Part No. 9997-37783-4

ISBN 0-15-332212-8 (Package of 12)

Reading and Language Skills Assessment Pretest

Timeless Treasures / Theme 4

Name _____ Date _____

SKILL AREA	Criterion Score	Pupil Score	Pupil Strength
VOCABULARY AND CONCEPTS Word Relationships	4/6	_____	_____
COMPREHENSION Text Structure: Compare and Contrast	6/8	_____	_____
LANGUAGE Comparing with Adjectives Main and Helping Verbs Action Verbs; Objects of Verbs Linking Verbs Simple Tenses; Present Tense	7/10	_____	_____
TOTAL SCORE	17/24	_____	_____

Were accommodations made in administering this test?   ☐ Yes   ☐ No

Type of accommodations: _____

_____

ISBN 0-15-332212-8

3 4 5 6 7 8 9 10   170   10 09 08 07 06 05 04 03 02

VOCABULARY AND CONCEPTS: Word Relationships

Directions: Read the passage. Fill in the answer circle in front of the correct answer for each question.

When the train conductor asked for her ticket, Natalie began to <u>fumble</u> in her purse to find it. "I'm sorry," she said, "but I seem to be in a bit of a <u>predicament</u>. I can't find my ticket. Is there any way you could help me with this problem?"

1. The word <u>fumble</u> in this passage means to _____.
   - Ⓐ lose your grip on a football
   - Ⓑ feel your way in the dark
   - Ⓒ succeed in a blundering way
   - Ⓓ search awkwardly for something

2. The word <u>predicament</u> in this passage means a _____.
   - Ⓐ closed space
   - Ⓑ part of a sentence
   - Ⓒ difficult situation
   - Ⓓ warning of future events

GO ON

VOCABULARY AND CONCEPTS: Word Relationships (continued)

Directions: Read each sentence. Fill in the answer circle in front of the correct answer for each question.

3. Read the sentence.

We will be late if we don't <u>board</u> the train.

In which sentence does the word <u>board</u> mean the same thing as in the sentence above?

Ⓐ I need to cut this <u>board</u> in half.

Ⓑ I have to <u>board</u> up the windows before the storm hits land.

Ⓒ The final whistle sounded to tell passengers to <u>board</u> the ship.

Ⓓ My parents pay for my sister's room and <u>board</u> at college.

4. Read the sentence.

I had to tear the coupon out of a magazine.

Which of these words in the sentence could be pronounced in two different ways and mean two different things?

Ⓐ had

Ⓑ tear

Ⓒ coupon

Ⓓ out

5. In which sentence is the underlined *homophone* used **incorrectly**?

Ⓐ I <u>sent</u> the letter by overnight mail.

Ⓑ There is a beautiful purple <u>flour</u> in the backyard.

Ⓒ The day grew dark as a black cloud blocked the <u>sun</u>.

Ⓓ The next step is to <u>pour</u> the milk into the mixing bowl.

6. How are the words *remote* and *distant* related?

Ⓐ They are synonyms.

Ⓑ They are antonyms.

Ⓒ They are homophones.

Ⓓ They are homographs.

STOP

COMPREHENSION: Text Structure: Compare and Contrast

Directions: Read each passage. Fill in the answer circle in front of the correct answer for each question.

There are three classes of fish living today: jawless fish, cartilage fish, and bony fish. Jawless fish are like eels. They have smooth skin without scales and round, jawless mouths. Their skeletons are made of cartilage, which is softer than bone. They live by eating dead fish or as parasites attached to living fish.

Cartilage fish are so named because their skeletons never change from cartilage to bone during development. A shark is a cartilage fish. Sharks have mouths with jaws and are expert predators. Their skin feels rough, like sandpaper, because it is covered with small toothlike bumps called *denticles*. Cartilage fish must keep swimming to stay afloat.

Bony fish, which include goldfish, tuna, and catfish, make up ninety-five percent of all fish. They have skeletons made of bone, and their bodies are covered by bony scales. Bony fish can stay afloat without swimming because they have a special balloonlike organ called a swim bladder. Meat-eating fish may eat worms, insects, crayfish, or other fish.

7. A way that jawless fish and cartilage fish are alike is that they both _____.
   Ⓐ have swim bladders
   Ⓑ live as parasites
   Ⓒ have cartilage skeletons
   Ⓓ are covered with denticles

GO ON

COMPREHENSION: Text Structure: Compare and Contrast (continued)

8. One difference between catfish and sharks is that catfish _____.
   - Ⓐ have jaws
   - Ⓑ look like eels
   - Ⓒ are very good predators
   - Ⓓ can stay afloat without swimming

9. Compared with jawless fish, bony fish _____.
   - Ⓐ are better parasites
   - Ⓑ exist in greater number
   - Ⓒ have fewer scales
   - Ⓓ have rounder mouths

10. Compared with jawless fish, cartilage fish _____.
   - Ⓐ have rougher, bumpier skin
   - Ⓑ look more like eels
   - Ⓒ have the same kind of jaws
   - Ⓓ have bonier skeletons

GO ON

Harcourt • Reading and Language Skills Assessment

COMPREHENSION: Text Structure: Compare and Contrast (continued)

Butterflies and moths belong to the *Lepidoptera* group of insects. The name *Lepidoptera* means "scaly wing." If you have ever touched the wing of one of these insects, you know that it feels dusty. This dust is made of the tiny scales that make up the wings' pattern. When the scales come off, you can see through the wing. It is hard to believe that these graceful creatures all start out as caterpillars in cocoons.

Butterflies almost always have brighter colors than moths. Their bodies are also thinner. The antennae on a butterfly are long and thin, and they have knobs on the ends. A moth's antennae look like tiny feathers. One other difference between moths and butterflies is that moths are usually active at night and butterflies are out in the daytime. Those insects flying around the porch light at night are moths, not butterflies.

Butterflies and moths come in many different sizes. Some are incredibly tiny, while one kind of butterfly has a wingspan of about eleven inches. Butterflies and moths are found all over the world, except for in Antarctica. Most are found in the tropics, because they can find food there all year long. Adult moths and butterflies drink nectar, which they usually find in flowers.

11. One way in which moths and butterflies are alike is that they both have _____.

Ⓐ the same bright colors

Ⓑ bodies with the same shape

Ⓒ wings made of tiny scales

Ⓓ antennae that resemble tiny feathers

GO ON

COMPREHENSION: Text Structure: Compare and Contrast (continued)

12. One difference between moths and butterflies is that only moths _____.
Ⓐ drink nectar
Ⓑ live all over the world
Ⓒ come in different sizes
Ⓓ are active at night

13. You would expect to find both moths and butterflies _____.
Ⓐ in the tropics
Ⓑ in Antarctica
Ⓒ around a porch light at night
Ⓓ developing in the same cocoons

14. You can most easily tell the difference between a moth and a butterfly by looking at its _____.
Ⓐ food
Ⓑ nectar
Ⓒ antennae
Ⓓ scales

STOP

Score _____

LANGUAGE

Directions: Choose the form of the **adjective** that best completes each sentence.

15. John is the _____ of the three brothers.
    - Ⓐ more small
    - Ⓑ most smaller
    - Ⓒ smallest
    - Ⓓ smaller

16. I think that science is a _____ subject than math or social studies.
    - Ⓐ more interest
    - Ⓑ most interestingest
    - Ⓒ most interesting
    - Ⓓ more interesting

17. Denise feels _____ because she has a fever and coughs frequently.
    - Ⓐ badly
    - Ⓑ bad
    - Ⓒ worst
    - Ⓓ badder

Directions: Choose the **helping verb** that best completes the verb phrase.

18. The lawyers _____ scheduled to meet with their client at 3 P.M. today.
    - Ⓐ are
    - Ⓑ can
    - Ⓒ is
    - Ⓓ has

19. Jasmine _____ bought small gifts for each of the guests at her party.
    - Ⓐ may
    - Ⓑ has
    - Ⓒ have
    - Ⓓ will

GO ON

LANGUAGE (continued)

Directions: Fill in the answer circle in front of the correct answer for each question.

20. Which answer correctly describes the underlined word in this sentence?

    Since we couldn't attend Anna's graduation, she is sending <u>us</u> pictures of the event.

    Ⓐ action verb
    Ⓑ linking verb
    Ⓒ direct object
    Ⓓ indirect object

21. The linking verb is underlined in this sentence. Which word is connected to the subject by the linking verb?

    The soup <u>tastes</u> rather salty, but I will eat it to please the person who made it.

    Ⓐ The
    Ⓑ salty
    Ⓒ please
    Ⓓ person

22. The linking verb is underlined in this sentence. Which word is connected to the subject by the linking verb?

    The small museum's prize relic <u>is</u> a gem-encrusted crown worn by an ancient king.

    Ⓐ small
    Ⓑ museum's
    Ⓒ crown
    Ⓓ king

GO ON

LANGUAGE (continued)

Directions: Choose the correct verb form to complete each sentence.

23. My sister _____ a heavy course load in college.
    - (A) carryes
    - (B) carryies
    - (C) carrys
    - (D) carries

24. As the runner turns the corner, she _____ the baton to another member of the relay team.
    - (A) pass
    - (B) passys
    - (C) passes
    - (D) passs

STOP

TROPHIES

Creative Solutions / Theme 4
Reading and Language Skills Assessment

Harcourt

Orlando   Boston   Dallas   Chicago   San Diego

Part No. 9997-37780-X

ISBN 0-15-332212-8 (Package of 12)

6

• T R O P H I E S •

Reading and Language Skills
Assessment Posttest

Timeless Treasures / Theme 4

Name _____ Date _____

SKILL AREA	Criterion Score	Pupil Score	Pupil Strength
VOCABULARY AND CONCEPTS Word Relationships	4/6	_____	_____
COMPREHENSION Text Structure: Compare and Contrast	6/8	_____	_____
LANGUAGE Comparing with Adjectives Main and Helping Verbs Action Verbs; Objects of Verbs Linking Verbs Simple Tenses; Present Tense	7/10	_____	_____
TOTAL SCORE	17/24	_____	_____

Were accommodations made in administering this test?   ❏ Yes   ❏ No

Type of accommodations: _____

_____

Harcourt • Reading and Language Skills Assessment

VOCABULARY AND CONCEPTS: Word Relationships

Directions: Read the passage. Fill in the answer circle in front of the correct answer for each question.

As soon as they walked into the party, Tony told his friend Luke that he wanted to <u>mill</u> around a little in the crowd. "I'll see you later when it's time to go home, OK?" Tony said as he walked away. "Some friend," Luke thought to himself. "I don't know anyone here, and now I don't even have Tony to talk to. I'm halfway <u>inclined</u> to leave right now before I change my mind."

1. The word <u>mill</u> in this passage means to _____.
   - Ⓐ grind into flour
   - Ⓑ cut grooves into a metal surface
   - Ⓒ wander randomly in a crowd of people
   - Ⓓ put a raised edge on a coin

2. The word <u>inclined</u> in this passage means _____.
   - Ⓐ drawn with a straightedge
   - Ⓑ having a slope
   - Ⓒ likely to do something
   - Ⓓ bowed or bent forward

GO ON

VOCABULARY AND CONCEPTS: Word Relationships (continued)

Directions: Read each sentence. Fill in the answer circle in front of the correct answer for each question.

3. Read the sentence.

My dad bought himself a new <u>set</u> of golf clubs.

In which sentence does the word <u>set</u> mean the same thing as in the sentence above?

Ⓐ The doctor carefully <u>set</u> the broken bone.

Ⓑ Mom will use her good <u>set</u> of dishes for the party.

Ⓒ My grandfather says that he is old and <u>set</u> in his ways.

Ⓓ The couple have yet to <u>set</u> a wedding date.

4. Read the sentence.

My watch doesn't have batteries, so I must wind it all the time.

Which of these words in the sentence could be pronounced in two different ways and mean two different things?

Ⓐ doesn't

Ⓑ have

Ⓒ must

Ⓓ wind

5. In which sentence is the underlined *homophone* used **incorrectly**?

Ⓐ I had <u>cereal</u> for breakfast this morning.

Ⓑ We finally had to <u>sell</u> our old car.

Ⓒ The wind <u>blue</u> all day long.

Ⓓ The bloodhound has a keen <u>sense</u> of smell.

6. How are the words *gradually* and *rapidly* related?

Ⓐ They are synonyms.

Ⓑ They are antonyms.

Ⓒ They are homophones.

Ⓓ They are homographs.

STOP

Score _____

Harcourt • Reading and Language Skills Assessment

Timeless Treasures / Theme 4

COMPREHENSION: Text Structure: Compare and Contrast

Directions: Read each passage. Fill in the answer circle in front of the correct answer for each question.

In the United States and many other countries, there are two very different kinds of trees. *Coniferous* trees, which are also called "evergreens," grow mostly in colder areas, although they can sometimes be found in warmer places as well. These trees include pine, fir, and spruce. *Deciduous* trees grow in many different places. These trees include oak and maple. Coniferous trees are sometimes called "softwoods," and deciduous trees are sometimes called "hardwoods."

Unlike coniferous trees, deciduous trees have broad leaves, which usually change colors and fall before winter arrives. Coniferous trees, on the other hand, have thin, needle-shaped leaves. They do not change colors or fall off in the autumn the way leaves of deciduous trees do.

Wood from coniferous trees is often used for making paper, for building homes, and for making wooden models. The reasons are as follows: Coniferous trees grow quickly, the lumber from them is easy to cut with tools and is lighter to carry, and the wood is a better insulator than hardwoods. Wood from deciduous trees is often used for furniture, especially fine furniture. The wood is usually more expensive than softwoods. Both kinds of wood can be burned in a fireplace, but hardwood is preferred because it burns longer and does not contain as much tar, which can clog up a chimney.

7. One way in which coniferous and deciduous trees are alike is that they both _____.

Ⓐ are called "evergreens"
Ⓑ turn colors in the fall
Ⓒ grow in the United States
Ⓓ lose their leaves each year

GO ON

COMPREHENSION: Text Structure: Compare and Contrast (continued)

8. One difference between hardwood and softwood is that hardwood is better for _____.

Ⓐ making paper

Ⓑ making models

Ⓒ building homes

Ⓓ making furniture

9. Compared to the wood from a deciduous tree, the wood from a coniferous tree is likely to be _____.

Ⓐ softer

Ⓑ heavier

Ⓒ more expensive

Ⓓ harder to cut with tools

10. According to this passage, you can tell the difference between coniferous trees and deciduous trees by looking at their _____.

Ⓐ grain

Ⓑ bark

Ⓒ leaves

Ⓓ roots

GO ON

Harcourt • Reading and Language Skills Assessment

COMPREHENSION: Text Structure: Compare and Contrast (continued)

Many people think monkeys and apes are the same animal. This is not correct. Monkeys and apes are classified by most scientists in the larger group of mammals known as *primates*. However, the ape family includes chimpanzees, gorillas, and orangutans. Apes tend to be larger than monkeys. Monkeys are divided into two groups: Old World monkeys and New World monkeys. These two groups look similar to each other, but they are found in different parts of the world. Baboons are Old World monkeys, while howler monkeys and spider monkeys are New World monkeys.

Most primates are good climbers. Their arms are almost always longer than their legs. They also have fingers and toes they can use for climbing and grasping. Apes have larger and more complex brains than monkeys. They are considered to be more intelligent animals. Some apes have even been taught to understand human language. Apes also stand upright some of the time. Unlike monkeys, apes do not have tails. Monkeys, on the other hand, often have long tails that they use for balance and swinging.

Apes are found only in tropical areas of Africa and Asia. They live in jungles, and their main diet is leaves and fruit. Monkeys are found all over the world, from Asia to Africa to Central and South America. Most monkeys live in trees in the forest, although some live in open country on the ground. They, too, eat mostly plants; some monkeys, however, eat insects or small reptiles. Many kinds of apes and monkeys are in danger of extinction as forests and jungles disappear.

11. One way in which monkeys and apes are alike is that both _____.

Ⓐ have tails

Ⓑ understand human language

Ⓒ may be in danger of extinction

Ⓓ live only in Africa and Asia

GO ON

COMPREHENSION: Text Structure: Compare and Contrast (continued)

12. One difference between monkeys and apes is that some monkeys _____.

Ⓐ are mammals

Ⓑ are primates

Ⓒ can grasp with their fingers

Ⓓ eat insects or small reptiles

13. Compared to a monkey, an ape is likely to _____.

Ⓐ have greater intelligence

Ⓑ spend more time in trees

Ⓒ be much smaller in size

Ⓓ swing more gracefully

14. According to the passage, orangutans are classified in the same family as _____.

Ⓐ New World monkeys

Ⓑ Old World monkeys

Ⓒ gorillas

Ⓓ baboons

STOP

Score _____

LANGUAGE

Directions: Choose the form of the **adjective** that best completes each sentence.

15. The candidate's current TV ad is _____ than last week's ad.

(A) good

(B) better

(C) best

(D) well

16. Stan is the _____ of all the students in my art class.

(A) creativest

(B) creaviter

(C) most creative

(D) more creative

16. Stan is the _____ of all the students in my art class.

17. When it comes to enforcing house rules, my father is _____ than my mother.

(A) lenient

(B) most lenient

(C) lenienter

(D) more lenient

Directions: Choose the **helping verb** that best completes the verb phrase.

18. The guest speaker _____ lecture on the dangers of global warming.

(A) do

(B) is

(C) have

(D) will

19. When you have finished your homework, you _____ play video games.

(A) are

(B) has

(C) may

(D) is

GO ON

LANGUAGE (continued)

Directions: Fill in the answer circle in front of the correct answer for each question.

20. Which answer correctly describes the underlined word in this sentence?

    The quarterback <u>threw</u> the football to the downfield receiver.

    Ⓐ action verb

    Ⓑ linking verb

    Ⓒ direct object

    Ⓓ indirect object

21. The linking verb is underlined in this sentence. Which word is connected to the subject by the linking verb?

    The Supreme Court <u>is</u> the final interpreter of the law in our nation.

    Ⓐ final

    Ⓑ interpreter

    Ⓒ law

    Ⓓ nation

22. The linking verb is underlined in this sentence. Which word is connected to the subject by the linking verb?

    The audience members <u>seemed</u> bored by the dialogue and poor acting in the play.

    Ⓐ bored

    Ⓑ dialogue

    Ⓒ acting

    Ⓓ play

GO ON

LANGUAGE (continued)

Directions: Choose the correct verb form to complete each sentence.

23. The artist first _____ an outline of her subject using charcoal.
    A sketchss
    B skechies
    C sketches
    D sketchs

24. The United States _____ most of the world's grain.
    A supplyes
    B supplyies
    C supplys
    D supplies

STOP

· T R O P H I E S ·

Creative Solutions / Theme 4
Reading and Language Skills Assessment

Harcourt

Orlando   Boston   Dallas   Chicago   San Diego

Part No. 9997-37774-5

ISBN 0-15-332212-8 (Package of 12)

6

· TROPHIES ·

Reading and Language Skills
Assessment Pretest

Timeless Treasures / Theme 5

Name _____ Date _____

SKILL AREA	Criterion Score	Pupil Score	Pupil Strength
COMPREHENSION			
Author's Purpose and Perspective	3/4	_____	_____
Draw Conclusions	6/8	_____	_____
LANGUAGE	7/10	_____	_____
Past and Future Tenses			
Principal Parts of Verbs			
Regular and Irregular Verbs			
Perfect Tenses			
Progressive Forms			
TOTAL SCORE	16/22	_____	_____

Were accommodations made in administering this test? ☐ Yes ☐ No

Type of accommodations: _____

_____

ISBN 0-15-332212-8

3 4 5 6 7 8 9 10   170   10 09 08 07 06 05 04 03 02

COMPREHENSION: Author's Purpose and Perspective

Directions: Read each passage. Fill in the answer circle in front of the correct answer for each question.

Author 1

A new volunteer program will soon be offered at Jefferson Middle School. Each Friday after school at 4:00 P.M., a bus will be available to take interested students to the Sunrise Nursing Home. At Sunrise, each student will be introduced to an elderly patient, who will be a "Friday Friend." The purpose of the visits is to bring cheer to the elderly, some of whom rarely receive visitors. Students may entertain their new friends with music (singing or playing an instrument), reading aloud, or just talking to share their feelings. Students who are interested in participating in the volunteer program should sign up in their homeroom classes.

Author 2

Sign up and join the fun! Jefferson Middle School is about to begin a fabulous new program of visits to the elderly. Every Friday after school at 4:00, you can hop on a bus and go to the Sunrise Nursing Home to visit with a special "Friday Friend." This is your chance to really make a difference in our community. You see, some of the people at Sunrise never get visitors. But you can solve that problem and give them something to look forward to—Friday visits from you! Can you imagine how happy it would make a lonely person feel if you took time each week to read or just talk with the person? And you'd get benefits, too. Just think how much you could learn about what life was like in the past. It's way more fun to learn from someone who's really lived an experience than it is to read about it in a textbook. Plus, if you have any problems, these people can give you advice. After all, they probably know a lot by now! This is a chance to help others, to help yourself, and to make a real contribution. Sign up today!

GO ON

COMPREHENSION: Author's Purpose and Perspective (continued)

1. The main purpose of Author 1 is to _____ .
   - (A) persuade
   - (B) inform
   - (C) entertain
   - (D) warn

2. Which of the following statements would most likely be used by Author 1?
   - (A) Please volunteer! It will be a great experience.
   - (B) Can you imagine how lonely you'd feel if no one ever visited you?
   - (C) The bus will bring you back to the school at 6:00 P.M.
   - (D) This experience will be so rewarding that you'll never forget it.

3. The main purpose of Author 2 is to _____ .
   - (A) persuade
   - (B) inform
   - (C) entertain
   - (D) warn

4. Which of the following statements would most likely be used by Author 2?
   - (A) To participate, you must have your parents sign a permission slip.
   - (B) This is a great way to hear some fantastic stories and make a new friend!
   - (C) Applications for the program must be submitted by the end of the week.
   - (D) The program will begin the first Friday of next month.

STOP

COMPREHENSION: Draw Conclusions

Directions: Read each passage. Fill in the answer circle in front of the correct answer for each question.

Not too many years ago, people had a lot of mistaken ideas about bats. They thought that all bats were scary creatures, like the ones they saw in horror movies. The more we learn about bats, though, the more popular they become. In fact, many people now build "bat houses" to attract bats to their yards.

There are almost 1,000 different kinds of bats around the world. The largest have wingspans up to 6 feet, while the smallest weigh less than a penny. Most are found in the tropics, although about 50 species live in North America. Bats are the only flying mammals. Some have short, wide wings, and others have long, narrow ones. Some can hover over flowers, while others can fly long distances to find food. Their wings and faces look different, depending on where they live and what they eat.

Many species of bats eat insects—lots and lots of insects. A single little brown bat can catch 1,200 mosquitoes in an hour! From one cave in Texas, 20 million Mexican free-tail bats eat 200 *tons* of insects every night. Other kinds of bats eat fruit, nectar from flowers, and even frogs and fish. During the day, bats usually rest upside-down in large groups in dark, quiet places. As night falls, they fly out together to find food. Bats navigate using a system called "echolocation." Each bat sends out high-pitched sounds that hit objects and are reflected back to the bat. The bat hears these sounds and can then tell whether the object is something to be avoided—such as a tree or another bat—or is food to be caught, such as a tasty moth.

GO ON

COMPREHENSION: Draw Conclusions (continued)

5. From the facts in the passage, it is reasonable to conclude that people might build bat houses so that the bats that come to live in them will _____ .

Ⓐ eat the fish in local ponds

Ⓑ frighten the neighbors

Ⓒ not have to live in caves anymore

Ⓓ eat insects around the people's homes

6. From the facts in the passage, it is reasonable to conclude that a bat's _____ help it navigate.

Ⓐ wings

Ⓑ ears

Ⓒ claws

Ⓓ skin

7. According to the passage, bats are in the same animal family as _____ .

Ⓐ worms

Ⓑ fish

Ⓒ mice

Ⓓ birds

8. According to the facts in the passage, it is reasonable to conclude that most bats are _____ .

Ⓐ vicious

Ⓑ useless

Ⓒ helpful

Ⓓ dangerous

Harcourt • Reading and Language Skills Assessment

GO ON

COMPREHENSION: Draw Conclusions (continued)

Pangolins are animals that live in tropical Asia and Africa. These creatures look like a cross between anteaters and armadillos. They are usually three to five feet long and weigh about ten to sixty pounds. They have long snouts, long tongues, and long tails. Interestingly, like American anteaters, pangolins are toothless. Their bodies are covered with overlapping brown-colored horny scales that are composed of cemented hairs.

If threatened, pangolins roll themselves into tight balls, making them look similar to coiled snakes. Their scales provide such a strong armor that few enemies can harm them. If they are captured, they are likely to lash out with their long, scaled tails.

Most species of pangolins live in trees, though some are ground dwellers and live in burrows. They feed on termites and ants, which they catch by thrusting out their long, sticky, ropelike tongues. Searching for food only at night, pangolins locate prey by smell and then use the long, sharp claws on their five-toed feet to rip open the nests of ants and termites.

9. According to the passage, if you found a pangolin rolled into a ball, it would mean that it is _____ .
   Ⓐ afraid of being attacked
   Ⓑ seriously wounded
   Ⓒ trying to attract a snake
   Ⓓ in a deep sleep

10. From the facts in the passage, it is reasonable to conclude that pangolins _____ .
   Ⓐ have a poor sense of smell
   Ⓑ swallow their food without chewing
   Ⓒ are defenseless when threatened
   Ⓓ sleep from sunset to sunrise

GO ON

COMPREHENSION: Draw Conclusions (continued)

> If you look at all the continents of the earth, they seem to fit together like pieces of a puzzle. In the early 1900s, a German meteorologist named Alfred Wegener presented a paper in which he expressed the opinion that the continents have moved great distances during the past 100 million years. Wegener put forth a theory that all the continents we know today were once a great, joined landmass, which he called *Pangaea*, which is Greek for "all land" or "all earth." He believed that Pangaea split apart during the time of the dinosaurs and that the continents then moved steadily in all directions to where they are now. This idea became known as "continental drift." The theory helped explain a lot of things, including why the continents fit together so neatly. Wegener spent the rest of his life defending his theory, which did not become commonly accepted until several decades after his death.

11. Which of these would have been most likely to have inspired the theory of continental drift?
    - (A) seeing a volcano erupt
    - (B) watching a lightning storm
    - (C) seeing an iceberg break apart from a glacier
    - (D) watching a meteorite hit the earth

12. Which of the following would best support the theory of continental drift?
    - (A) finding fossils of unique plant and animal species on both sides of the Atlantic Ocean
    - (B) discovering a rich concentration of minerals on a continent
    - (C) discovering that a continent has a great number of mammals that burrow into the ground
    - (D) finding that a continent has many renewable sources of energy, such as wood or water

STOP

Score _____

LANGUAGE

Directions: Choose the verb form or verb tense that best completes each sentence.

13. Can you believe the bodybuilder actually _____ the phone book in half?

Ⓐ rip

Ⓑ riped

Ⓒ ripped

Ⓓ rippied

14. We _____ inside the nearest building to avoid the pelting rain.

Ⓐ hurrying

Ⓑ hurryed

Ⓒ burryied

Ⓓ hurried

15. In class yesterday, we _____ an interesting video about animals and plants in tropical rain forests.

Ⓐ will be watching

Ⓑ watch

Ⓒ will watch

Ⓓ watched

16. In the past two years, the champion race-car driver _____ some of the world's fastest cars.

Ⓐ drives

Ⓑ has driven

Ⓒ will drive

Ⓓ will be driving

GO ON

LANGUAGE (continued)

---

17. The biologists are _____ how water pollution affects animal life.

Ⓐ studyed

Ⓑ studied

Ⓒ studying

Ⓓ study

18. By this time tomorrow evening, the playoff game _____ .

Ⓐ begin

Ⓑ began

Ⓒ is beginning

Ⓓ will have begun

GO ON

Timeless Treasures / Theme 5

Harcourt • Reading and Language Skills Assessment

LANGUAGE (continued)

Directions: Read each sentence. Then choose the answer that best describes the underlined verb or verb phrase.

19. The veterinarian is <u>watching</u> the animal's wound for signs of infection.
    - Ⓐ present
    - Ⓑ present participle
    - Ⓒ past
    - Ⓓ past participle

20. The scientists <u>debated</u> whether water is present on the planet Mars.
    - Ⓐ present
    - Ⓑ present participle
    - Ⓒ past
    - Ⓓ past participle

21. By 7 P.M. this evening, my father's train <u>will have arrived</u>.
    - Ⓐ present perfect tense
    - Ⓑ past perfect tense
    - Ⓒ future perfect tense
    - Ⓓ future progressive form

22. Jesse asked me to go to the movies, but I <u>had</u> already <u>told</u> Tamika that we would go skating.
    - Ⓐ present perfect tense
    - Ⓑ past perfect tense
    - Ⓒ future perfect tense
    - Ⓓ past progressive form

STOP

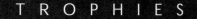· T R O P H I E S ·

Making a Difference / Theme 5
Reading and Language Skills Assessment

Harcourt

Orlando   Boston   Dallas   Chicago   San Diego

Part No. 9997-37781-8

ISBN 0-15-332212-8 (Package of 12)

6

Reading and Language Skills Assessment Posttest

Timeless Treasures / Theme 5

Name _____ Date _____

SKILL AREA	Criterion Score	Pupil Score	Pupil Strength
COMPREHENSION			
Author's Purpose and Perspective	3/4	_____	_____
Draw Conclusions	6/8		
LANGUAGE Past and Future Tenses Principal Parts of Verbs Regular and Irregular Verbs Perfect Tenses Progressive Forms	7/10	_____	_____
TOTAL SCORE	16/22	_____	_____

Were accommodations made in administering this test? ❑ Yes ❑ No

Type of accommodations: _____

_____

COMPREHENSION: Author's Purpose and Perspective

Directions: Read each passage. Fill in the answer circle in front of the correct answer for each question.

Author 1

Reminder: Student Council elections will be held tomorrow during second period. Ballot forms will be distributed at the beginning of the period and collected at the end. Students will have a chance to vote for a class president, vice-president, treasurer, and secretary for each grade level. There are also five at-large Student Council seats for each grade level. Candidates for president of each class will present speeches at an assembly in the auditorium today after lunch. Each candidate will have five minutes to speak.

Author 2

My name is Lamar Reyes, and I would like to be your class president. Five minutes is not long enough to list all the reasons you should vote for me, but I'll give it a try. First of all, I am reliable. If I say I am going to do something, I do it. Second, I get along with everyone. I like to have fun, but I am serious, too. I have been active in several school clubs, including the Service Club and the Outdoor Club. I am also on the soccer team. But the main reason you should vote for me is that I have good ideas for improving our school. If I am elected, our class will raise money to plant shade trees by the outdoor tables. Everyone knows it is too hot to sit out there at the beginning and end of the school year. We will also have canned food drives twice a year to donate to the Food Bank. And finally, we will start an after-school tutoring program in the library for students who need extra help with their homework. So as you cast your ballot tomorrow, remember me, Lamar Reyes. You'll be glad you did!

GO ON

COMPREHENSION: Author's Purpose and Perspective (continued)

1. The main purpose of Author 1 is to _____.
   (A) entertain
   (B) inform
   (C) persuade
   (D) warn

2. Which of the following statements would most likely be used by Author 1?
   (A) Candidates for other offices will not make speeches.
   (B) So, don't forget to cast your ballot for your favorite candidate!
   (C) Of course, Student Council does not have any real power.
   (D) Vote wisely—the choices you make will greatly affect your life!

3. The main purpose of Author 2 is to _____.
   (A) entertain
   (B) inform
   (C) persuade
   (D) describe

4. Which of the following statements would most likely be used by Author 2?
   (A) Lunch period will be shortened by five minutes.
   (B) I am a candidate who will really make a difference.
   (C) Second period begins at 8:55 and ends at 9:40.
   (D) The winners of the election will be announced tomorrow.

STOP

Score _____
Timeless Treasures / Theme 5

Harcourt • Reading and Language Skills Assessment

COMPREHENSION: Draw Conclusions

Directions: Read each passage. Fill in the answer circle in front of the correct answer for each question.

On May 18, 1980, the top of Mount St. Helens blew off in a violent explosion. The volcano in Washington State had been peaceful for hundreds of years. Then, a few months before it erupted, small earthquakes shook the mountain. Steam rose out of cracks along its top and sides. A bulge began to grow in the side of the mountain. Every day the bulge grew larger and more frightening.

On May 18 there was another earthquake. This one shook the bulge loose and sent huge boulders tumbling down the mountainside. Out of the hole shot steam, ash, and rocks from the fiery insides of the earth at the speed of a hurricane! Mud and rocks raced down the mountain, filling streams and lakes. All the ice and snow melted at once, adding to the flow. Ash rose into the sky and fell to the ground hundreds of miles away. In some places the ash turned the sky as dark as night.

The blast killed millions of trees and thousands of animals, insects, and plants. It made major changes to the landscape. On the top there was now a crater instead of a peak. There were no more forests or lakes, and mud and ash covered everything.

Many people were surprised to see that animals and plants soon returned to Mount St. Helens. Even large animals like elk began to come back only a few weeks after the eruption. The mountain is still not as beautiful as it was before that day in May, but there is life on it.

GO ON

COMPREHENSION: Draw Conclusions (continued)

5. From the facts in the passage, it is reasonable to conclude that the materials which shot out of the bulge were all very _____.

Ⓐ hot

Ⓑ large

Ⓒ soft

Ⓓ wet

6. From the facts in the passage, it is reasonable to conclude that for months before May 18, 1980, _____.

Ⓐ the mountain looked odd

Ⓑ the mountain had no wildlife on it

Ⓒ more people than usual visited the mountain

Ⓓ pressure was building up inside the mountain

7. According to the passage, it is reasonable to conclude that the blast completely and permanently changed the mountain's _____.

Ⓐ location

Ⓑ shape

Ⓒ climate

Ⓓ name

8. According to the facts in the passage, the mountain now looks as if it is _____.

Ⓐ taller

Ⓑ unchanged

Ⓒ recovering

Ⓓ unable to support life

GO ON

Harcourt • Reading and Language Skills Assessment

COMPREHENSION: Draw Conclusions (continued)

Leonardo da Vinci is considered one of the greatest artists, scientists, and inventors who ever lived. He was born in Italy in 1452. His talent as a painter was clear when he was only 15 years old. When Leonardo's teacher saw how beautiful his paintings were, the teacher decided never to paint again.

As a young man Leonardo went to work for the Duke of Milan. At that time wealthy people paid artists to create their art. The Duke paid Leonardo to paint and make sculptures, but he also asked him to design weapons, buildings, and machines. Over the next 17 years, Leonardo made plans for flying machines, submarines, tanks, and many other inventions. He also designed canals, bridges, and churches. Many of these things were never built, but Leonardo's detailed drawings remain. He spent a lot of time studying nature. He also studied human beings so that he could draw and sculpt them better.

Leonardo was so busy that he did not finish all the projects he started. One painting that he did finish was the Mona Lisa, which is now in a museum in Paris, France. It is probably the most famous painting ever created.

After the Duke lost his power in 1499, Leonardo worked for many different people. The last person he worked for was King Francis I of France. The king paid Leonardo well and gave him a large house. The king was by his side when Leonardo died in 1519.

GO ON

COMPREHENSION: Draw Conclusions (continued)

9. From the facts in the passage, it is reasonable to conclude that a number of Leonardo's ideas for inventions and machines would have been used for _____.
   Ⓐ fighting wars
   Ⓑ making clothing
   Ⓒ sending messages
   Ⓓ healing illnesses

10. From the facts in the passage, it is reasonable to conclude that King Francis I of France thought of Leonardo as a _____.
   Ⓐ silly fool
   Ⓑ close friend
   Ⓒ dangerous enemy
   Ⓓ casual acquaintance

11. According to the passage, Leonardo's art teacher found the boy's talent to be _____.
   Ⓐ awe-inspiring
   Ⓑ disappointing
   Ⓒ overrated
   Ⓓ ordinary

12. According to the passage, in the 1400s most artists were dependent upon _____.
   Ⓐ popularity with the general public
   Ⓑ government funding
   Ⓒ rich supporters
   Ⓓ loans from family members

STOP

Score _____

Harcourt • Reading and Language Skills Assessment

LANGUAGE

Directions: Choose the verb form or verb tense that best completes each sentence.

13. The inventor _____ greatly from the sale of his latest invention.
    - Ⓐ profittyied
    - Ⓑ profittied
    - Ⓒ profityed
    - Ⓓ profited

14. The robbery _____ at 6 P.M. yesterday.
    - Ⓐ occurried
    - Ⓑ occuryed
    - Ⓒ occurred
    - Ⓓ occured

15. Over the past six months, the attorney _____ evidence that will free his client.
    - Ⓐ gathers
    - Ⓑ has gathered
    - Ⓒ will gather
    - Ⓓ will be gathering

16. I called out to my dad, but he couldn't hear me because he _____ the lawn.
    - Ⓐ was mowing
    - Ⓑ mowed
    - Ⓒ will mow
    - Ⓓ mow

GO ON

LANGUAGE (continued)

17. By the end of this month, the trees _____ to bloom.
    (A) begin
    (B) began
    (C) is beginning
    (D) will have begun

18. I _____ on inviting twenty guests to my party, but I only invited fifteen.
    (A) plan
    (B) will plan
    (C) had planned
    (D) will be planning

LANGUAGE (continued)

Directions: Read each sentence. Then choose the answer that best describes the underlined verb or verb phrase.

19. David was so tired that he <u>slept</u> until noon.
- (A) present
- (B) present participle
- (C) past
- (D) past participle

20. By sundown, the campers <u>had pitched</u> their tents and had begun to cook dinner.
- (A) present
- (B) present participle
- (C) past
- (D) past participle

21. By the time we reach our destination, we <u>will have driven</u> 1,000 miles.
- (A) present perfect tense
- (B) past perfect tense
- (C) future perfect tense
- (D) past progressive form

22. My class <u>is collecting</u> canned food to donate to the Food Bank.
- (A) present perfect tense
- (B) past perfect tense
- (C) future perfect tense
- (D) present progressive form

STOP

TROPHIES

Making a Difference / Theme 5
Reading and Language Skills Assessment

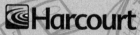

Harcourt

Orlando   Boston   Dallas   Chicago   San Diego

Part No. 9997-37775-3

ISBN 0-15-332212-8 (Package of 12)

6

• T R O P H I E S •

Reading and Language Skills Assessment Pretest

Timeless Treasures / Theme 6

Name _____ Date _____

SKILL AREA	Criterion Score	Pupil Score	Pupil Strength
VOCABULARY AND CONCEPTS			
Denotation/Connotation	3/4	_____	_____
COMPREHENSION			
Text Structure:			
Cause and Effect	3/4	_____	_____
Fact and Opinion	3/4	_____	_____
LANGUAGE	7/10	_____	_____
Contractions and Negatives			
Adverbs			
Comparing with Adverbs			
Prepositional Phrases			
Adjective and Adverb Phrases			
TOTAL SCORE	16/22	_____	_____

Were accommodations made in administering this test? ❑ Yes ❑ No

Type of accommodations: _____

_____

ISBN 0-15-332212-8

3 4 5 6 7 8 9 10   170   10 09 08 07 06 05 04 03 02

VOCABULARY AND CONCEPTS: Denotation/Connotation

Directions: Fill in the answer circle in front of the correct answer for each question.

1. In which sentence does the underlined word have the most **positive** connotation?
   Ⓐ Karen felt enraptured after earning a good grade on her math test.
   Ⓑ Karen felt satisfied after earning a good grade on her math test.
   Ⓒ Karen felt happy after earning a good grade on her math test.
   Ⓓ Karen felt pleased after earning a good grade on her math test.

2. In which sentence does the underlined word have the most **positive** connotation?
   Ⓐ With the right amount of water and sunlight, the rose bushes grew.
   Ⓑ With the right amount of water and sunlight, the rose bushes flourished.
   Ⓒ With the right amount of water and sunlight, the rose bushes matured.
   Ⓓ With the right amount of water and sunlight, the rose bushes developed.

3. In which sentence does the underlined word have the most **negative** connotation?
   Ⓐ The presentation the visitor gave to the class was thorough.
   Ⓑ The presentation the visitor gave to the class was long-winded.
   Ⓒ The presentation the visitor gave to the class was lengthy.
   Ⓓ The presentation the visitor gave to the class was wordy.

4. In which sentence does the underlined word have the most **negative** connotation?
   Ⓐ After winning the race, the girl was filled with pride.
   Ⓑ After winning the race, the girl was filled with confidence.
   Ⓒ After winning the race, the girl was filled with arrogance.
   Ⓓ After winning the race, the girl was filled with satisfaction.

STOP

COMPREHENSION: Text Structure: Cause and Effect

Directions: Read the passage. Fill in the answer circle in front of the correct answer for each question.

George Eastman invented many things to help people take pictures. He was born into a poor family in New York. As a young man, he worked in a bank. When it was time to take a vacation, he wanted to take pictures of the things he would see.

However, this was not so easy long ago. In the 1870s, cameras did not use film. Instead, cameras used glass plates coated with chemicals. Also, a picture had to be developed right after it was taken. If you wanted to take pictures, you had to carry a lot of equipment.

So Eastman started experimenting. He had read that in England, the camera plates were dry. He invented his own dry plates. Soon he left his job at the bank to open a dry-plate business. His business did very well, but photographers were not happy with the dry plates. Eastman experimented some more and came up with the idea of film. In 1888, he invented a small camera. He also invented film that was rolled up on a spool.

Photographers could take pictures and then send the camera back to Eastman's company to be developed. Eastman made up the name "Kodak" for the new camera. The famous inventor Thomas A. Edison ordered a Kodak camera. He used it to invent the motion picture camera, so that we now have movies. George Eastman became very rich from his inventions. He donated lots of money to schools and charities.

GO ON

Harcourt • Reading and Language Skills Assessment

COMPREHENSION: Text Structure: Cause and Effect (continued)

5. In the 1870s, why would it have been difficult for George Eastman to take pictures on his vacation?
   - Ⓐ Eastman didn't own his own camera.
   - Ⓑ A lot of equipment was needed to take and develop pictures.
   - Ⓒ Eastman rarely took vacations because his family needed his income.
   - Ⓓ Cameras were not allowed on vacation trips back then.

6. Why did Eastman leave his job in a bank?
   - Ⓐ He was more interested in inventing cameras and film.
   - Ⓑ The manager of the bank did not like him.
   - Ⓒ He could not make enough money in a bank to support himself.
   - Ⓓ He had trouble adding and subtracting numbers.

7. Why would photographers buy cameras from Eastman, take pictures, and then send the cameras back to him?
   - Ⓐ They wanted to try another inventor's cameras.
   - Ⓑ They could exchange old cameras for modern ones.
   - Ⓒ Eastman's cameras did not work properly.
   - Ⓓ Eastman developed their pictures.

8. What did Thomas Edison create by using one of Eastman's cameras?
   - Ⓐ modern printing presses
   - Ⓑ phonographs
   - Ⓒ lightbulbs
   - Ⓓ motion pictures

STOP

COMPREHENSION: Fact and Opinion

Directions: Read the passage. Fill in the answer circle in front of the correct answer for each question.

At the school carnival next week, our class will have a booth where foods from different cultures can be purchased. No one could ever think of a better idea for a booth than that. Since Maria's family is from Mexico, her mother is going to make fresh tortillas to sell at the booth. Maria is also going to bring guacamole, marinated grilled meat, pico de gallo, and cheese. People can put those in the tortillas to make fajitas. Everyone will love those. Tony is of Italian descent, so he and his grandmother are making big pans of lasagna. Just the smell of lasagna makes everyone hungry. Karl's ancestors came from Germany. In their honor, he and his dad are going to grill bratwurst. People will be able to buy bratwurst, hot mustard, and sauerkraut. That's the best meal on earth, if you ask me. Lian and her aunt are going to bring dim sum with hoisin sauce. It's impossible not to love Chinese food. Finally, Kai is going to make teriyaki steak, a dish served often in Hawaii. When it's cooked, she'll cut it up, put bite-size chunks on skewers, and serve it with rice. Now *that* sounds delicious. It's impossible for anyone to like any booth better than ours. Our booth idea is the best in the whole school.

GO ON

COMPREHENSION: Fact and Opinion (continued)

9. Which of these is an **opinion** from the passage?
   - Ⓐ Our class will have a booth where foods from different cultures can be purchased.
   - Ⓑ Maria's mother is going to make fresh tortillas to sell at the booth.
   - Ⓒ That's the best meal on earth, if you ask me.
   - Ⓓ Lian and her aunt are going to bring dim sum with hoisin sauce.

10. Which of these is a **fact** from the passage?
   - Ⓐ No one could ever think of a better idea for a booth than that.
   - Ⓑ Karl's ancestors came from Germany.
   - Ⓒ Everyone will love those.
   - Ⓓ Just the smell of lasagna makes everyone hungry.

11. Which of these is an **opinion** from the passage?
   - Ⓐ It's impossible not to love Chinese food.
   - Ⓑ Tony and his grandmother are making big pans of lasagna.
   - Ⓒ Karl and his dad are going to grill bratwurst.
   - Ⓓ Kai is going to make teriyaki steak.

12. Which of these is a **fact** from the passage?
   - Ⓐ Now *that* sounds delicious.
   - Ⓑ People will be able to buy bratwurst, hot mustard, and sauerkraut.
   - Ⓒ It's impossible for anyone to like any booth better than ours.
   - Ⓓ Our booth idea is the best in the whole school.

STOP

LANGUAGE

Directions: Fill in the answer circle in front of the correct answer for each question.

13. Which is the correct **contraction** to replace the underlined words in this sentence?

    <u>We have</u> promised to look after our neighbor's plants while she is traveling.

    Ⓐ We'll

    Ⓑ We'd

    Ⓒ We've

    Ⓓ We're

14. Which sentence does **not** contain a double negative?

    Ⓐ Do not never go swimming if an adult is not present.

    Ⓑ Our basketball team hasn't never made it to the playoffs before.

    Ⓒ We couldn't scarcely hear over the sound of the car engine.

    Ⓓ The movie had hardly begun before the small child started to cry.

15. Choose the underlined word that is an **adverb** in this sentence.

    The <u>experienced</u> captain <u>easily</u> maneuvered the <u>large</u> <u>ship</u> into port.

    Ⓐ experienced

    Ⓑ easily

    Ⓒ large

    Ⓓ ship

GO ON

Timeless Treasures / Theme 6

LANGUAGE (continued)

16. Choose the underlined word that is an **adverb** in this sentence.

I was <u>very</u> <u>happy</u> to learn that my <u>favorite</u> cousin was coming for a two-week <u>visit</u>.

Ⓐ very   Ⓑ happy

Ⓒ favorite   Ⓓ visit

17. Choose the form of the **adverb** that correctly completes this sentence.

Bob is not the most talented athlete, but he works _____ than anyone.

Ⓐ most hardest   Ⓑ hardest

Ⓒ harder   Ⓓ more hard

18. Choose the form of the **adverb** that correctly completes this sentence.

The new telescope allows scientists to see objects in space _____ than ever before.

Ⓐ more clearly   Ⓑ most clearly

Ⓒ clear   Ⓓ more clear

19. Choose the word that is the **object** of the preposition in the prepositional phrase in this sentence.

The politicians repeatedly cheered and clapped during the president's lengthy speech.

Ⓐ politicians

Ⓑ repeatedly

Ⓒ lengthy

Ⓓ speech

20. Choose the word that is the **object** of the preposition in the prepositional phrase in this sentence.

A majestic bald eagle soared through the sky as tourists took pictures.

Ⓐ majestic

Ⓑ soared

Ⓒ sky

Ⓓ took

GO ON

LANGUAGE (continued)

Directions: Read each pair of sentences. Then choose the answer that shows the best way to combine the sentences into one sentence that includes the underlined adverb phrase.

21. Anita will meet Candi. They will meet <u>at the park</u>.

   Ⓐ Anita will meet Candi they will meet at the park.

   Ⓑ Anita and Candi at the park, will meet.

   Ⓒ Anita will meet Candi at the park.

   Ⓓ Anita at the park will meet Candi.

22. Bats came rushing out. They came <u>out of the cave's mouth</u>.

   Ⓐ Bats they came rushing came out of the cave's mouth.

   Ⓑ Bats came rushing out of the cave's mouth.

   Ⓒ Bats came rushing, out of the cave, of the mouth.

   Ⓓ Bats out of the cave's mouth, came rushing.

STOP

Expanding Worlds / Theme 6
Reading and Language Skills Assessment

Harcourt

Orlando   Boston   Dallas   Chicago   San Diego

Part No. 9997-37782-6

ISBN 0-15-332212-8 (Package of 12)

6

TROPHIES

Reading and Language Skills
Assessment Posttest

Timeless Treasures / Theme 6

Name _____ Date _____

SKILL AREA	Criterion Score	Pupil Score	Pupil Strength
VOCABULARY AND CONCEPTS			
Denotation/Connotation	3/4	_____	_____
COMPREHENSION			
Text Structure:			
Cause and Effect	3/4	_____	_____
Fact and Opinion	3/4	_____	_____
LANGUAGE	7/10	_____	_____
Contractions and Negatives			
Adverbs			
Comparing with Adverbs			
Prepositional Phrases			
Adjective and Adverb Phrases			
		_____	_____
TOTAL SCORE	16/22		

Were accommodations made in administering this test?   ❑ Yes   ❑ No

Type of accommodations: _____

_____

ISBN 0-15-332212-8

3 4 5 6 7 8 9 10   170   10 09 08 07 06 05 04 03 02

VOCABULARY AND CONCEPTS: Denotation/Connotation

Directions: Fill in the answer circle in front of the correct answer for each question.

1. In which sentence does the underlined word have the most **positive** connotation?
   Ⓐ John's performance in the band concert was <u>passable</u>.
   Ⓑ John's performance in the band concert was <u>acceptable</u>.
   Ⓒ John's performance in the band concert was <u>exceptional</u>.
   Ⓓ John's performance in the band concert was <u>adequate</u>.

2. In which sentence does the underlined word have the most **positive** connotation?
   Ⓐ Mrs. Hernandez is always <u>gracious</u> to her guests.
   Ⓑ Mrs. Hernandez is always <u>polite</u> to her guests.
   Ⓒ Mrs. Hernandez is always <u>kind</u> to her guests.
   Ⓓ Mrs. Hernandez is always <u>nice</u> to her guests.

3. In which sentence does the underlined word have the most **negative** connotation?
   Ⓐ The boy's answer to his mother was rather <u>abrupt</u>.
   Ⓑ The boy's answer to his mother was rather <u>brief</u>.
   Ⓒ The boy's answer to his mother was rather <u>simple</u>.
   Ⓓ The boy's answer to his mother was rather <u>limited</u>.

4. In which sentence does the underlined word have the most **negative** connotation?
   Ⓐ The manager of the office is quite <u>agreeable</u>.
   Ⓑ The manager of the office is quite <u>spineless</u>.
   Ⓒ The manager of the office is quite <u>compliant</u>.
   Ⓓ The manager of the office is quite <u>accommodating</u>.

STOP

Score _____

COMPREHENSION: Text Structure: Cause and Effect

Directions: Read each passage. Fill in the answer circle in front of the correct answer for each question.

The Grand Canyon in Arizona is the largest canyon in the world, and one of the most beautiful. It is 277 miles long, up to 18 miles wide, and 1 mile deep. The canyon began to form less than 10 million years ago, when an uplift in the land made the Colorado River run faster. The river carries rocks of different sizes that bounce along the riverbed. As they tumble along, the rocks scrape the bottom, making it deeper and deeper. There is very little rain in this part of the country, so the land on the surface does not wear away. That is why, bit by bit, the canyon walls became steeper.

As the canyon grew deeper, older and older layers of rock were exposed. These rocks were formed between 600 million and 200 million years ago. Each layer contains the fossils of different plants and animals that lived during that period. The fossils help scientists learn what the world was like at that time. At the bottom of the canyon are some of the earth's oldest exposed rocks. They were formed such a long time ago that no fossils are found in them.

Today there are dams on the Colorado River that control the flow of water into the Grand Canyon. The river still cuts into the earth, but more slowly than it did before. Even so, a thousand years from now the Grand Canyon will not look the same as it did when people first discovered it.

5. Which first caused the Grand Canyon to begin forming?
   - Ⓐ An uplift in the land made a river run faster.
   - Ⓑ Heavy rains wore away the surface of the land.
   - Ⓒ Rocks scraped away the bottom of a riverbed.
   - Ⓓ Plants and animals wore away a trail in the land.

6. What effect have dams had on the Grand Canyon and the Colorado River?
   - Ⓐ They have caused the river to cut more deeply into the earth.
   - Ⓑ They have caused the river to cut more quickly into the earth.
   - Ⓒ They have slowed the rate at which the river cuts into the earth.
   - Ⓓ They have stopped the river from cutting any farther into the earth.

GO ON

Harcourt • Reading and Language Skills Assessment

COMPREHENSION: Text Structure: Cause and Effect (continued)

The smallest of the world's penguins live on Phillip Island, Australia. These Little Penguins, as they are called, are only half the size of the penguins that live in Antarctica. In January 2000, an oil spill near the island put these little creatures in danger. An oil spill can destroy the natural oil in penguins' feathers. Then they have no protection from the cold water. Penguins also clean and smooth their feathers with their beaks. If they swallow the poisonous oil, they could die.

People working in the Phillip Island Nature Park wanted to save the birds from the oil spill. Then someone came up with a good idea. After the volunteers cleaned the birds, they dressed them in doll sweaters. Then the penguins were put in special pools to get their strength back. The wool sweaters kept the penguins warm and stopped them from swallowing the oil on their feathers.

Knitters from all over the world heard about the project. They sent tiny sweaters with bows on them. Other people sent sweaters in the colors of different sports teams. Everyone agreed the penguins looked cute. Only their heads and flippers stuck out of the sweaters.

As the penguins swam, the salt water destroyed the wool. When the sweaters were gone, the birds were ready to go back into the ocean. Their own natural oil had come back, so they would be warm enough to survive.

7. Oil can cause penguins to die from poisoning or from _____.
   (A) starvation
   (B) freezing
   (C) disease
   (D) heatstroke

8. What caused the little sweaters to be destroyed?
   (A) The penguins outgrew them.
   (B) The volunteers cut them into pieces.
   (C) The oil caused them to shrink.
   (D) The salt water dissolved the wool.

STOP

COMPREHENSION: Fact and Opinion

Directions: Read the passage. Fill in the answer circle in front of the correct answer for each question.

Our class is trying to decide where to go for our spring trip. Exactly half the kids voted to go to the amusement park, and the other half voted to go to the lake. Of course, everyone loves roller coasters, so that's a good reason to go to the amusement park. The tilt-a-whirl ride is too scary, though. The amusement park would cost more, but I'm sure we could raise the money somehow. There are a lot of exciting things to do at the lake, too. There's a softball field there, and we could divide into teams and play ball. If it rains, there is also a covered picnic area by the lake, but most places in the amusement park aren't covered. The lake is absolutely beautiful in the spring. Fruit trees around the lake are in bloom at that time of year. If we go to the amusement park, we couldn't take our own lunches because they don't let you take food in. If we go to the lake, we could take food to cook on the grills and have a picnic. Food cooked outdoors is the best! We could even bring an old-fashioned ice-cream maker and make our own dessert. The ice cream they sell at the amusement park is really good, too. Nothing tastes better than ice cream after you've been going on the rides all day. It's clear that this decision is going to be difficult to make!

Harcourt • Reading and Language Skills Assessment

GO ON

COMPREHENSION: Fact and Opinion (continued)

9. Which of these is an **opinion** from the passage?
   Ⓐ Our class is trying to decide where to go.
   Ⓑ Half the kids voted to go to the amusement park.
   Ⓒ The other half voted to go to the lake.
   Ⓓ Everyone loves roller coasters.

10. Which of these is a **fact** from the passage?
   Ⓐ The amusement park would cost more.
   Ⓑ I'm sure we could raise the money somehow.
   Ⓒ There are a lot of exciting things to do at the lake.
   Ⓓ The lake is absolutely beautiful in the spring.

11. Which of these is an **opinion** from the passage?
   Ⓐ There's a softball field at the lake.
   Ⓑ The tilt-a-whirl ride is too scary.
   Ⓒ We could divide into teams and play ball.
   Ⓓ There is a covered picnic area by the lake.

12. Which of these is a **fact** from the passage?
   Ⓐ This decision is going to be difficult to make!
   Ⓑ Nothing tastes better than ice cream.
   Ⓒ Fruit trees around the lake will be in bloom.
   Ⓓ Food cooked outdoors is the best!

STOP

LANGUAGE

Directions: Fill in the answer circle in front of the correct answer for each question.

13. Which is the correct **contraction** to replace the underlined words in this sentence?

    The foreman for the construction crew said that <u>they will</u> be working around the clock until the job is finished.

    (A) they'll

    (B) they're

    (C) they'd

    (D) they've

14. Which sentence does **not** contain a double negative?

    (A) We couldn't scarcely see through the mist that hugged the ground.

    (B) Not nobody in our family has ever traveled to Europe.

    (C) Hardly anyone attended the free concert by our symphony.

    (D) I hadn't never considered a career in medicine until my counselor suggested it.

15. Choose the underlined word that is an **adverb** in this sentence.

    The <u>newest</u> applicant for the job of <u>city</u> manager is <u>barely</u> <u>qualified</u>.

    (A) newest

    (B) city

    (C) barely

    (D) qualified

GO ON

Harcourt • Reading and Language Skills Assessment

LANGUAGE (continued)

16. Choose the underlined word that is an **adverb** in this sentence.

The <u>excited</u> scientist <u>carefully</u> <u>examined</u> the <u>fragments</u> of fossilized bone.

Ⓐ excited

Ⓑ carefully

Ⓒ examined

Ⓓ fragments

17. Choose the form of the **adverb** that correctly completes this sentence.

My father travels _____ than he did on his previous job.

Ⓐ frequently

Ⓑ most frequently

Ⓒ more frequent

Ⓓ more frequently

18. Choose the form of the **adverb** that correctly completes this sentence.

Of all the new medicines, the latest experimental drug acts _____
to cure infections.

Ⓐ most rapid

Ⓑ most rapidly

Ⓒ more rapidly

Ⓓ rapidly

19. Choose the word that is the **object** of the preposition in the prepositional phrase in this sentence.

The gardener planted beautiful rosebushes along the curved sidewalk.

Ⓐ beautiful

Ⓑ rosebushes

Ⓒ along

Ⓓ sidewalk

GO ON

LANGUAGE (continued)

20. Choose the word that is the **object** of the preposition in the prepositional phrase in this sentence.

The policemen jumped into their car and drove rapidly away.

(A) policemen

(B) into

(C) car

(D) rapidly

Directions: Read each pair of sentences. Then choose the answer that shows the best way to combine the sentences into one sentence that includes the underlined adverb phrase.

21. Mark was going shopping. He was going <u>with his mother</u>.

(A) Mark was going shopping, going with his mother.

(B) Mark was going shopping with his mother.

(C) Mark with his mother were going, shopping.

(D) Mark was going shopping, his mother was going.

22. Jana found her bracelet. It was <u>under a sofa cushion</u>.

(A) Jana found her bracelet under a sofa cushion.

(B) Jana under a sofa cushion, found her bracelet.

(C) Jana found under a sofa cushion, her bracelet.

(D) Jana found her bracelet, was under a sofa cushion.

STOP

Expanding Worlds / Theme 6
Reading and Language Skills Assessment

Orlando Boston Dallas Chicago San Diego

Part No. 9997-37776-1

ISBN 0-15-332212-8 (Package of 12)

· TROPHIES ·

End-of-Year Reading and Language Skills Assessment

Timeless Treasures / Themes 1–6

Name _____ Date _____

SKILL AREA	Criterion Score	Pupil Score	Pupil Strength
VOCABULARY AND CONCEPTS	6/8	_____	_____
COMPREHENSION	12/16	_____	_____
LITERARY RESPONSE AND ANALYSIS	6/8	_____	_____
RESEARCH AND INFORMATION SKILLS	3/4	_____	_____
LANGUAGE	10/14	_____	_____
TOTAL SCORE	37/50		

Were accommodations made in administering this test?   ❑ Yes   ❑ No

Type of accommodations: _____

_____

Printed in the United States of America

ISBN 0-15-332212-8

3 4 5 6 7 8 9 10   170   10 09 08 07 06 05 04 03 02

VOCABULARY AND CONCEPTS

Directions: Fill in the answer circle in front of the correct answer for each question.

1. **Please deactivate the alarm system.**

   What does the word *deactivate* mean?
   Ⓐ activate again
   Ⓑ the opposite of activate
   Ⓒ wrongly activate
   Ⓓ activate halfway

2. Which root means *good*?
   Ⓐ "mitt" as in **transmittal**
   Ⓑ "sign" as **design**
   Ⓒ "bene" as in **benevolent**
   Ⓓ "ology" as in **zoology**

3. Read the sentence.

   Grandfather made this chair from a single <u>block</u> of wood.

   In which sentence does the word <u>block</u> mean the same thing as in the sentence above?
   Ⓐ I couldn't life the heavy <u>block</u> of ice.
   Ⓑ Please do not <u>block</u> the emergency exits.
   Ⓒ My best friend lives down the <u>block</u> from me.
   Ⓓ The play's director has yet to <u>block</u> the actor's movements.

4. Read the sentence.

   During the hiking trip, my father was always in the lead.

   Which of these words in the sentence could be pronounced in two different ways and mean two different things?
   Ⓐ the
   Ⓑ hiking
   Ⓒ always
   Ⓓ lead

VOCABULARY AND CONCEPTS (continued)

5. In which sentence is the underlined *homophone* used **incorrectly**?

Ⓐ The farmer carried the milk in a <u>pail</u>.

Ⓑ There were <u>four</u> students absent from class.

Ⓒ My <u>feat</u> are sore from all that running.

Ⓓ There is only one main <u>road</u> in our small town.

6. How are the words *dependable* and *reliable* related?

Ⓐ They are synonyms.

Ⓑ They are antonyms.

Ⓒ They are homophones.

Ⓓ They are homographs.

7. In which sentence does the underlined word have the most **positive** connotation?

Ⓐ When Bill saw the Grand Canyon, he was <u>interested</u>.

Ⓑ When Bill saw the Grand Canyon, he was <u>awestruck</u>.

Ⓒ When Bill saw the Grand Canyon, he was <u>pleased</u>.

Ⓓ When Bill saw the Grand Canyon, he was <u>impressed</u>.

8. In which sentence does the underlined word have the most **negative** connotation?

Ⓐ Gene felt sorry for the elderly man dressed in <u>old</u> clothes.

Ⓑ Gene felt sorry for the elderly man dressed in <u>plain</u> clothes.

Ⓒ Gene felt sorry for the elderly man dressed in <u>ragged</u> clothes.

Ⓓ Gene felt sorry for the elderly man dressed in <u>simple</u> clothes.

Harcourt • Reading and Language Skills Assessment

COMPREHENSION

Directions: Read each passage. Fill in the answer circle in front of the correct answer for each question.

Hundreds of years ago, different Indian tribes lived in different kinds of dwellings. Each type of "housing" depended to a large extent on the Indians' lifestyle and the area of the country in which they lived. The best dwellings appeared along the Northwest Coast.

The Hopi Indians lived in the Southwest, where hot days were often followed by cold nights, and periods of drought could be broken by heavy rains and flooding. They lived in *pueblos*—adobe houses built next to or even on top of each other. The Hopis used ladders to enter their houses. Hopi families lived in one room, sleeping on blankets rolled out on the floor. The Navajos of the Southwest lived in cone-shaped houses called *hogans*. The hogans were log frames covered with mud or grass. They were built in small, family-sized groups miles apart from each other. Building the hogans far apart was clever because it allowed for privacy.

The Chinooks lived in the Northwest Coast along the Pacific Ocean—an area filled with rivers and forests. Their villages were made up of rows of long wooden houses with no windows. Each house was built partly over a hole in the ground so that some rooms were actually under the ground. Several families lived in each of these *pit houses*. The families in each house belonged to the same clan, which means that they were related to each other. It's easier to live with other families if you're related to them.

The Cherokees lived in the Eastern Woodlands of North America. They made their homes in rich river valleys. Cherokee families had two houses. One house was used for warmth during the winter; the other was used to stay cool during the hot summer months. The winter houses were small, cone-shaped pit houses made of wooden poles covered with earth. The summer houses were larger. They were shaped like boxes and had grass or clay walls and bark roofs. Several families of the same clan lived together in these summer and winter houses. Cherokees built their houses close together to form villages. Sometimes a Cherokee village might have as many as 300–400 houses.

The Kiowas of the Great Plains were nomads, always traveling from place to place. They followed buffalo herds across the flat grasslands. Because they followed the buffalo, the Kiowas built shelters that could be moved quickly and easily. One kind of shelter they lived in was a cone-shaped tent, or *tepee*, made of wooden poles set in a circle and covered with buffalo skins. They also used buffalo skins for their beds and blankets. These skins were probably more comfortable to sleep on than blankets.

Harcourt • Reading and Language Skills Assessment

COMPREHENSION (continued)

9. One way that the dwellings of the Kiowas were different from those of the Cherokees is that the dwellings of the Kiowas were _____.

   (A) entered by ladders

   (B) easy to move quickly

   (C) under the ground

   (D) built on top of each other

10. Which of these is an **opinion** from the passage?

    (A) The Navajos of the Southwest lived in cone-shaped houses called *hogans*.

    (B) The Cherokees' summer houses had grass or clay walls and bark roofs.

    (C) Building the hogans far apart was clever because it allowed for privacy.

    (D) The Kiowas followed buffalo herds across the flat grasslands.

11. Which of these is a **fact** from the passage?

    (A) The best dwellings appeared along the Northwest Coast.

    (B) These skins were probably more comfortable to sleep on than blankets.

    (C) It's easier to live with other families if you're related to them.

    (D) Sometimes a Cherokee village might have as many as 300–400 houses.

12. One way that the dwellings of the Cherokees and the Chinooks were the same is that they both _____.

    (A) housed several families from the same clan

    (B) were small and shaped like cones

    (C) were built on flat grasslands

    (D) had clay walls and bark roofs

13. The purpose of this passage is to _____.

    (A) persuade

    (B) inform

    (C) entertain

    (D) warn

Harcourt • Reading and Language Skills Assessment

COMPREHENSION (continued)

A couple of years ago, in 1872, Vance's father had decided to move their family from the East to a 160-acre plot of land on the Great Plains. During the two years since the move, the family had endured many hardships, but they were also beginning to feel at home in their new surroundings. Because trees were scarce, they had built their house out of *sod*, which is earth cut into blocks and held together with grass and roots. The house kept them cool in the summer and warm in the winter, but it was not without its shortcomings. When it rained, water leaked through the roof. In the summer, when it was hot and dry, the roof baked, causing dust and dirt to fall from the ceiling onto the furniture below. Vance's mother said she had her hands full just trying to keep the house clean enough to live in. Still, their corn and potato crops had done well this past year, and they had plenty to eat. Their well also supplied them with plenty of water for drinking and washing. They were comfortably settled in, for now.

This particular hot, late-summer day, Vance's father and mother had left him in charge of the homestead while they made a trek to the closest town to buy supplies. They left at sunrise, warning Vance that they might not make it back home before dark. Vance was to do his chores and stay close to the house.

About three in the afternoon, while Vance was out in the field plucking ears of sweet corn to cook for supper, the sky began to grow dark. A strong wind blew in, and Vance heard thunder rumbling. As he studied the sky, he also saw jagged streaks of lightning in the distance. Gathering up the corn he had picked, he hurried into the house. About fifteen minutes later, Vance stepped back outside. The storm had blown over, and the air was still. Scanning the horizon, Vance spotted an orange glow not too far away. For a moment he couldn't figure out what it was, but suddenly he realized that it was fire. Lightning must have struck the dry prairie grasses, setting them ablaze. The hot summer days with no rain had left the surrounding acres as dry as tinder. The fire would sweep across the plains rapidly. Forcing down panic, Vance's mind raced as he tried to think what he should do to save the house—and himself.

COMPREHENSION (continued)

14. Vance is alone at home on this late-summer day because his parents _____.

   (A) have gone back East to visit relatives

   (B) are helping a neighbor build a sod house

   (C) have gone to town to buy supplies

   (D) are selling their corn and potatoes at a market

15. Why does Vance leave the fields and hurry inside the house?

   (A) He wants to clean the house before his mother gets home.

   (B) He sees a storm that seems to be coming his way.

   (C) He remembers his parents said he was to stay inside.

   (D) He wants to cook supper before it gets dark.

16. What causes the grasses near Vance's home to catch fire?

   (A) Lightning strikes the dry fields.

   (B) A child plays carelessly with matches.

   (C) A camper does not put out his campfire.

   (D) A neighbor burning brush loses control of his fire.

17. The purpose of this passage is to _____.

   (A) persuade

   (B) inform

   (C) entertain

   (D) warn

COMPREHENSION (continued)

The atmosphere surrounding the earth is a thin layer of gases. The atmosphere makes life possible on earth. It allows light to reach the surface of the earth to supply energy and to make photosynthesis possible. It also radiates some heat back to the earth to warm our planet.

The atmosphere is made up of individual layers, one of which is called the *stratosphere*. The stratosphere contains the ozone layer, which protects living things on Earth from the sun's harmful ultraviolet (UV) radiation.

In 1985, a British scientific journal published some alarming information. An article in the journal reported the results of studies conducted by scientists on the coast of Antarctica. Their studies showed that the ozone layer above the South Pole had become at least 50 to 98 percent thinner than it had been twenty years previously. After these results were published, NASA scientists studied data sent back to Earth by a weather satellite that was launched in 1978. The scientists also saw signs of ozone thinning.

This thinning of the protective ozone layer is a serious matter. As the amount of ozone in the stratosphere decreases, more harmful ultraviolet light reaches the surface of the earth. This UV light can cause a host of problems for humans. It can cause skin cancer as well as faster aging. It can cause eye cataracts that blur vision or lead to blindness. Our immune systems can even be weakened by too much ultraviolet light, making it more difficult for us to ward off diseases. Additionally, one-celled organisms living near the surface of the ocean can be killed by too much UV light, which could alter ocean food chains and result in reduced fish harvests. Excessive UV light can also cause lower crop yields by interfering with photosynthesis.

All countries of the earth can be affected by this thinning of the ozone layer. To address the problem, many of the world's countries have agreed to restrict or ban the use of substances that pose a significant danger to the ozone layer. However, harmful substances used years ago can stay active in the stratosphere for as long as 50 to 100 years. It will take many years for the ozone layer to recover.

COMPREHENSION (continued)

18. What is the main idea of this passage?
   (A) The atmosphere surrounding the earth is a thin layer of gases.
   (B) The thinning of the ozone layer is a serious matter that can cause many problems for humans.
   (C) The atmosphere allows light to reach the earth to supply energy and radiates heat to warm our planet.
   (D) The atmosphere is made up of individual layers, one of which is called the *stratosphere*.

19. Which detail could best be added to this passage?
   (A) Ocean currents are caused by winds and the rotation of the earth.
   (B) Air currents swirling in the troposphere can carry dry, frigid air from the Arctic.
   (C) Commercial airliners often fly in the lower stratosphere.
   (D) Exposure to harmful UV light can cause wrinkles and damaged skin.

20. From the facts in this passage, it is reasonable to conclude that _____.
   (A) studies showing that the ozone layer has thinned above the South Pole have little significance for other areas of the earth
   (B) protection of the ozone layer is a worldwide concern that requires international cooperation
   (C) scientific journals published in Britain are more reliable than those published in the United States
   (D) the protective ozone layer could quickly and easily be restored if a few large countries would ban harmful substances

21. The author has given you enough evidence to lead you to believe that _____.
   (A) losing the protective ozone layer could cause serious health problems and reductions in the world's food supply
   (B) the coast of Antarctica is the only valid place to retrieve data about the ozone layer
   (C) changes in the thickness of the ozone layer will not affect crop production
   (D) data showing decreases in the ozone layer are interesting but should not be a cause for serious concern or alarm

COMPREHENSION (continued)

You have probably learned in your science classes that there are nine planets, including our own Earth, in orbit around our sun. Astronomers, who study planets and other bodies in space, often divide the planets in our solar system into two groups. The "inner planets" include Mercury, Venus, Earth, and Mars. They are the planets closest to the sun, and they share several common characteristics.

For example, the inner planets are smaller than the other planets (except Pluto). The diameter of Mercury (the smallest of the four inner planets) is about 4,878 kilometers. The diameter of Earth (the largest of the four) is about 12,756 kilometers. These numbers sound big until you compare them to the diameters of the "outer planets," which range from 49,528 kilometers for Neptune to 142,984 kilometers for Jupiter! Pluto's diameter is only about 2,320 kilometers, but Pluto is a "strange duck" in many ways. Some have argued that it isn't even a planet.

Another major difference involves temperature. The surface of Mercury is about 175°C, but Venus is even hotter; Earth's surface is about 15°C, while that of Mars is –55°C. In contrast, temperatures on the outer planets range from –110°C on Jupiter to about –230°C on Pluto.

Still another difference involves the materials the planets are made of. The inner planets, such as Earth, are mostly made of hard materials such as iron and nickel at their cores. The outer planets are apparently made mostly of gases. These planets are less dense than the inner planets even though they are larger.

COMPREHENSION (continued)

22. What is one way in which all nine planets in our solar system are alike?
    - (A) They are equally dense.
    - (B) They are about the same size.
    - (C) They orbit around the sun.
    - (D) They are made of the same materials.

23. One difference between the outer planets and the inner planets is that the outer planets are _____.
    - (A) smaller
    - (B) colder
    - (C) more solid
    - (D) closer to Earth

24. Which planet is apparently least like the other nine?
    - (A) Mercury
    - (B) Earth
    - (C) Jupiter
    - (D) Pluto

LITERARY RESPONSE AND ANALYSIS

Directions: Read each passage. Fill in the answer circle in front of the correct answer for each question.

Athena, the daughter of Zeus, was the goddess of wisdom. The city of Athens was named after her, and it was her chosen seat—her own city. One of her duties was to preside over the ornamental arts of women, such as spinning, weaving, and needlework.

In the course of her duties, a contest took place. A young maiden named Arachne was quite skilled in the arts of weaving and embroidery. This mortal had achieved great fame for her beautiful works. It was a pleasure to watch how skillfully she did her spinning and weaving. It was as if she had been taught by Athena herself. She could not bear, though, to be thought a pupil, even of a goddess. "Let Athena try her skill with mine," she declared. "If beaten, I will pay the penalty."

Athena heard this and was displeased. She assumed the form of an old woman and visited Arachne to give her some advice. "I have had much experience," she said. "You may challenge your fellow mortals, but do not compete with a goddess. I hope you will not despise my words."

Arachne stopped her spinning and look at the old woman in anger. "Keep your advice. I am not afraid of the goddess; let her try her skill, if she dare." Upon hearing this, Athena threw off her disguise and challenged Arachne to a contest.

They took turns weaving. Athena created a beautiful piece with scenes of the gods and the gods' reactions to mortals who had displeased or defied them. Undaunted, Arachne created an even more beautiful weaving that showed the failings and errors of the gods.

After seeing the beauty of Arachne's labor, Athena flew into a rage. She struck down the loom and touched the forehead of Arachne to make her feel guilt and shame. "Guilty woman," Athena cursed, "you and your descendants will preserve the memory of this lesson." Arachne's form shrank, her head grew smaller, and her fingers cleaved to her side and served as legs. The rest of her became a body out of which she spins her thread. Athena had transformed Arachne into a spider.

Harcourt • Reading and Language Skills Assessment

LITERARY RESPONSE AND ANALYSIS (continued)

25. This myth most likely takes place in _____.
    - Ⓐ modern days
    - Ⓑ ancient times
    - Ⓒ the Middle Ages
    - Ⓓ the future

26. Arachne could best be described as _____.
    - Ⓐ lighthearted and humorous
    - Ⓑ shy and withdrawn
    - Ⓒ skillful and stubborn
    - Ⓓ bold and incompetent

27. What arouses Athena's anger?
    - Ⓐ Zeus expels her from the city of Athens.
    - Ⓑ A wise old woman gives her advice.
    - Ⓒ Somebody steals her weavings.
    - Ⓓ Arachne thinks she is more skillful than Athena.

28. How is the problem in the myth resolved?
    - Ⓐ Athena has Arachne continue her spinning in the form of a spider.
    - Ⓑ Athena rewards Arachne by making her a goddess.
    - Ⓒ Zeus takes pity on Arachne and saves her from Athena's wrath.
    - Ⓓ Arachne is forced to stop weaving and to leave Athens forever.

LITERARY RESPONSE AND ANALYSIS (continued)

Directions: Read each sentence. Fill in the answer circle in front of the correct answer for each question.

29. My car intentionally quit working this morning, just to spite me. It must hate me!

    This is an example of _____.

    Ⓐ a metaphor

    Ⓑ a simile

    Ⓒ personification

    Ⓓ hyperbole

30. The high-speed train is like a bullet.

    This is an example of _____.

    Ⓐ a metaphor

    Ⓑ a simile

    Ⓒ personification

    Ⓓ hyperbole

LITERARY RESPONSE AND ANALYSIS (continued)

Directions: Read the passage. Fill in the answer circle in front of the correct answer for each question.

The air was still and hot. My small apartment was an oven. I sat next to an open window, hoping, praying for a breeze to stir the air. My body was like the wilted plant on the windowsill—tired and limp. My wet hair stuck to the sides of my face. I would have slept, but it was too hot. Then, the thin curtains began to move. I saw the flash of lightning, followed by loud thunder. Rain began to fall, and fresh air filled the room. I stuck my head out the window and laughed.

31. Which group of words in this passage is a simile?

Ⓐ My body was like the wilted plant . . .

Ⓑ My wet hair . . .

Ⓒ . . . the thin curtains . . .

Ⓓ . . . followed by loud thunder.

32. Which group of words in this passage is a metaphor?

Ⓐ The air was still and hot.

Ⓑ My small apartment was an oven.

Ⓒ Rain began to fall . . .

Ⓓ I stuck my head out the window and laughed.

Harcourt • Reading and Language Skills Assessment

RESEARCH AND INFORMATION SKILLS

Directions: Study the map and table below. Then fill in the answer circle in front of the correct answer for each question.

Top Wheat-Producing States in 1998 (in millions of bushels)	
Kansas	494.9
North Dakota	310.7
Oklahoma	198.9
Montana	168.8
Washington	157.4
Texas	136.5
South Dakota	120.8
Colorado	103.7
Idaho	102.4
Minnesota	80.4

Top Wheat-Producing States of 1998

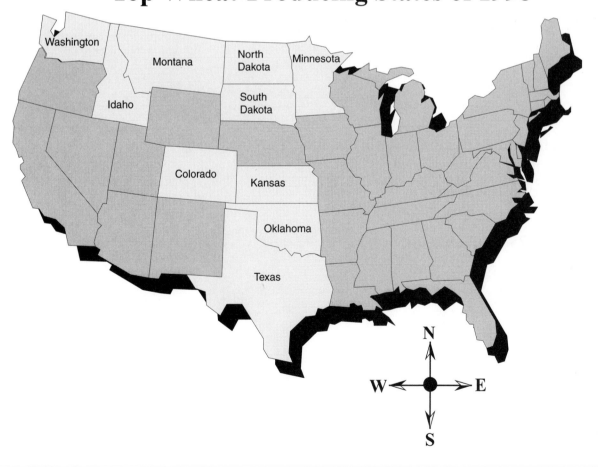

RESEARCH AND INFORMATION SKILLS (continued)

33. The top three wheat-producing states of 1998 are in what part of the country?

  Ⓐ Northeast

  Ⓑ Central

  Ⓒ West

  Ⓓ Southeast

34. Which state listed below is **not** one of the top wheat-producing states of 1998?

  Ⓐ Idaho

  Ⓑ Colorado

  Ⓒ Nebraska

  Ⓓ Texas

35. According to the map, how many of the top wheat-producing states of 1998 are south of Idaho?

  Ⓐ 1

  Ⓑ 4

  Ⓒ 10

  Ⓓ 17

36. How much more wheat did Oklahoma produce in 1998 than South Dakota produced?

  Ⓐ 78.1 bushels

  Ⓑ 80.4 bushels

  Ⓒ 78.1 million bushels

  Ⓓ 414.5 million bushels

LANGUAGE

Directions: Choose the answer that best describes the underlined words in each sentence.

37. <u>If we want to be on time for the movie,</u> we must leave now.
- Ⓐ independent clause
- Ⓑ complex sentence
- Ⓒ compound sentence
- Ⓓ dependent clause

38. The people who attended the street festival left lots of trash, but <u>city workmen quickly cleaned up the mess.</u>
- Ⓐ independent clause
- Ⓑ complex sentence
- Ⓒ compound sentence
- Ⓓ dependent clause

Directions: Choose the form of the **adjective** or **adverb** that best completes each sentence.

39. My parents' suitcases weigh a lot, but mine is the _____ of all.
- Ⓐ most heaviest
- Ⓑ more heavy
- Ⓒ heavier
- Ⓓ heaviest

40. I can barely keep up with my brother because he walks _____ than I do.
- Ⓐ rapidest
- Ⓑ more rapidly
- Ⓒ rapider
- Ⓓ more rapid

LANGUAGE (continued)

Directions: Choose the answer that correctly describes the underlined word in this sentence.

41. The principal gave <u>us</u> a stern lecture about misbehaving in class.
(A) action verb
(B) linking verb
(C) direct object
(D) indirect object

Directions: The linking verb is underlined in this sentence. Which word renames the subject of the sentence?

42. Alexander the Great <u>was</u> a skilled general who conquered much of the ancient world.
(A) skilled
(B) general
(C) much
(D) world

Harcourt • Reading and Language Skills Assessment

LANGUAGE (continued)

Directions: Read each sentence. Then choose the answer that best describes the underlined verb or verb phrase.

43. A crowd <u>gathered</u> in the park to watch the fireworks display.
   Ⓐ present
   Ⓑ present participle
   Ⓒ past
   Ⓓ past participle

44. By 6:30 A.M., Roy <u>had delivered</u> most of his newspapers.
   Ⓐ present perfect tense
   Ⓑ past perfect tense
   Ⓒ future perfect tense
   Ⓓ future progressive form

45. The members of the drama club <u>will be rehearsing</u> all week.
   Ⓐ present perfect tense
   Ⓑ past perfect tense
   Ⓒ future perfect tense
   Ⓓ future progressive form

LANGUAGE (continued)

Directions: Choose the **verb** or **verb phrase** that best completes each sentence.

46. Citizens _____ gathering signatures for a petition to be given to the mayor.
- Ⓐ can
- Ⓑ is
- Ⓒ are
- Ⓓ have

47. We _____ the heavy canoe downriver to avoid the dangerous rapids.
- Ⓐ carries
- Ⓑ carryed
- Ⓒ carryied
- Ⓓ carried

48. Roberto's skill as a writer _____ over the past several months.
- Ⓐ have grown
- Ⓑ has grown
- Ⓒ grows
- Ⓓ will grow

Directions: Choose the word that is the **object** of the preposition in the prepositional phrase in this sentence.

49. The doe and her fawn quickly disappeared into the thick brush.
- Ⓐ quickly
- Ⓑ into
- Ⓒ thick
- Ⓓ brush

LANGUAGE (continued)

Directions: Read this pair of sentences. Then choose the answer that shows the best way to combine the sentences into one sentence that includes the underlined adverb phrase.

50. Kendra received an e-mail. The e-mail was <u>from her cousin</u>.

Ⓐ Kendra and her cousin received her cousin's e-mail.

Ⓑ Kenra received an e-mail, it was from her cousin.

Ⓒ Kendra received an e-mail from her cousin.

Ⓓ Kendra received an e-mail; her cousin's e-mail.

STOP

Timeless Treasures / Themes 1–6
End-of-Year Reading and Language Skills Assessment

Harcourt

on   Dallas   Chicago   San Diego

Part No. 9997-37784-2

ISBN 0-15-332212-8 (Package of 12)